T0320799

The Pursuit of Happiness

The Pursuit of Happiness

Philosophical and Psychological Foundations of Utility

LOUIS NARENS AND BRIAN SKYRMS

OXFORD
UNIVERSITY PRESS

OXFORD
UNIVERSITY PRESS

Great Clarendon Street, Oxford, OX2 6DP,
United Kingdom

Oxford University Press is a department of the University of Oxford.
It furthers the University's objective of excellence in research, scholarship,
and education by publishing worldwide. Oxford is a registered trade mark of
Oxford University Press in the UK and in certain other countries

© Louis Narens and Brian Skyrms 2020

The moral rights of the authors have been asserted

First Edition published in 2020

Impression: 2

Published in the United States of America by Oxford University Press
198 Madison Avenue, New York, NY 10016, United States of America

British Library Cataloguing in Publication Data

Data available

Library of Congress Control Number: 2020935469

ISBN 978-0-19-885645-0

Printed and bound by
CPI Group (UK) Ltd, Croydon, CR0 4YY

In memory of R. Duncan Luce, friend and colleague, whose ideas and foundational research on utility theory, measurement, and psychophysics form the invisible backbone of this work.

Contents

PART II. MEASUREMENT AND PSYCHOPHYSICS

PART III. INTERPERSONAL COMPARISONS
AND CONVENTION

Preface

Men and women, like other animals, seek pleasure and avoid pain. If one wished to govern them according to their nature, one might aim to maximize pleasure and avoid pain. This idea was developed by the English Utilitarians as a plan for radical reform of government and law. The motto was to maximize the sum of pleasure minus pain.

This book does not argue whether this view is morally right or wrong. Rather it deals with the question as to whether the view has any clear meaning at all, and if so what it is. You can hardly evaluate an ethical doctrine without knowing what it means, but there is a tendency in moral philosophy to do just that. Jeremy Bentham, the central founding figure, worried about the measurement of pleasure and pain, and had some constructive things to say about it; his successors, with a few notable exceptions, were somewhat less worried. Pleasure and pain are treated as clear enough to propose examples and counterexamples and draw conclusions, while postponing the question of meaning. We believe that this is a mistake.

Economists have treated the question with various degrees of skepticism. Some have viewed the Utilitarian aggregate utility as quite meaningless. They see its ethical pronouncements, beyond "it would be good to make everyone happier (if you could)", as empty. But there is also now an attempt to resuscitate Utilitarianism based on contemporary neuroscience.

We approach this question of meaning from the overlapping perspectives of a cognitive scientist and a philosopher of science. We examine its history, paying attention to psychophysics old and new, measurement theory, positivism, expected utility theory, and contemporary neurobiology. Then, in the final chapters, we make new contributions of our own. A modification of ideas of the nineteenth-century Utilitarian and economist Edgeworth via measurement theory allows, in some favorable cases, meaningful aggregation of utility for a group. This aggregation is not, however, by taking the sum of utilities across people. Conventions of interpersonal comparison may be generated by an equilibration dynamics, and they may serve a socially beneficial purpose in coordinating group decisions.

Louis Narens
Brian Skyrms
4 November 2019

List of Figures

1

The Pursuit of Happiness

Preview

Utilitarianism, as we know it, began as movement for social reform based on our common humanity, and indeed on our common animality. Nature endows animals with systems of pleasure and pain to guide them through their lives. Pursuit of pleasure and avoidance of pain is just doing what comes naturally. If we are looking for a measure of group welfare, what could be more natural than to base it on an aggregate of the pleasures and pains of its members? As an ideology for social reform, Utilitarianism was remarkably effective. But the nagging question of how to measure individual and population utility persisted.

Jeremy Bentham worried about these questions because he wanted to make ethics a science. He said different things in different places, but we focus on two constructive ideas. The first is that sensations of individual pleasure and pain are to be measured by counting just noticeable differences (JNDs), a method of measurement based on increments of discrimination of pleasure; the second is that different kinds of pleasure sensations that are not directly measurable in this way are to be put on the same scale using preferences. Likewise, different modalities of pain are put on the same scale. Finally, preferences are to be used to put pleasure and pain of an individual on the same scale. None of this was worked out in any detail, but it is a remarkably rich set of ideas. There was an interplay between the two strands of thought, hedonic value and preference. Later Utilitarians and economists separated these. Regarding meaningful interpersonal comparisons, however, Bentham was a private skeptic, even if a public advocate.

Contemporaneous psychophysics has developed means to measure quantities of sensation to establish psychophysical laws, connecting quantities of physical stimulus with perceived sensational experiences. The method of just noticeable differences was adopted for this purpose, and other techniques involving direct measurement of subjective experience were developed later. Just as Bentham wanted to turn ethics into a science, the nineteenth-century

The Pursuit of Happiness: Philosophical and Psychological Foundations of Utility. Louis Narens and Brian Skyrms, Oxford University Press (2020). © Louis Narens and Brian Skyrms.
DOI: 10.1093/oso/9780198856450.001.0001

psychophysicist Gustav Theodor Fechner wanted to turn psychology into a science. He and later twentieth-century psychophysicists achieved this. Some psychophysicists were Utilitarians in ethics; some Utilitarians, notably the nineteenth-century economist Francis Ysidro Edgeworth, appealed to psychophysics in support of Utilitarianism.

Practitioners and critics of psychophysics began to look more closely at the details of JND that Bentham glossed over. Are comparisons of JND across different sensory modalities possible, and if so, what do they mean? Are there subliminal sensations that can't be counted so easily, but that have a cumulative effect? Is the idea that just noticeable differences are equally spaced just a convention, rather than a factual statement? Do the different ways of measuring JND (e.g., using different probability cutoffs) yield consistent results? Some of these questions are philosophical, and some are empirical. Most of the psychophysical experiments at the time were not done on pleasure at all, but on other sensations. The experiments that were done on pleasure in the nineteenth century seemed to point to a different psychophysical function, an inverted U-shape, from those in other domains, where the function was modeled as logarithmic or power. Some of the questions that were raised had to wait for future generations of psychologists for answers. Some are still waiting.

Some economists came to the conclusion that sensations of pleasure and pain could not be meaningfully measured at all, and thus focused on market behavior. The choice of an alternative from a set of alternatives was all that mattered to economics. For them, utilities were merely ordinal, Only the ordering of utilities mattered, because it determined choice behavior. If economics was to be made a science, it had to be purged of psychology.

These debates were often carried out in an informal manner, in the absence of a nuanced theory of different kinds of measurement and correlative senses of scientific meaningfulness. Measurement was thought of like measurement of length or mass in physics. A rigorous formal theory of measurement for psychology and economics had to wait for the twentieth century, when psychologists, philosophers, and mathematicians collaborated to produce what was required. The idea of invariance was imported from mathematics to make precise the notion of meaningfulness. In particular, scales of measurement such as interval scales, which fall between what previously were thought of as cardinal scales and ordinal scales, were introduced.

In the 1940s, John von Neumann and Oskar Morgenstern developed a measurement procedure that made sense of the utilities used in the payoff matrices of their theory of games. The expected utility principle was used to measure utilities of chance lotteries over prospects. Starting only with coherent preferences over such lotteries—an ordinal notion—they showed the existence of utilities measurable on an interval scale. Interval scales are determined only up to arbitrary choices of zero and unit, but that is all they need. An expected utility maximizer will choose the same if her scale is transformed by an arbitrary choice of zero point and unit. While previous economists, who dealt with choices over certain outcomes, could argue that only the order of utilities was relevant, Von Neumann and Morgenstern could argue that for expected utility maximizers, an interval scale of expectations is exactly what was needed.

So far so good, but suppose what is meaningful is that which is invariant over arbitrary independent changes of zero and of unit on the scales of individuals making up a group. Then almost all of what philosophers have said about Utilitarianism, pro and con, is quite *meaningless*. For group utility comparisons, we are left with only the idea of Pareto dominance. One social state Pareto dominates another if the first makes some better off and none worse off, according to their individual utility scales. This is a purely ordinal notion. Von Neumann and Morgenstern advanced the individual measurement question, but not the interpersonal comparability problem.

This was left to John Harsanyi, working within the Von Neumann-Morgenstern utility framework. Suppose individuals have utilities, measurable on interval scales. And we want to have group utilities, arising from coherent group preferences over the same lotteries, in the same way. Suppose the group utilities—given a choice of zero and unit for the group—are not the sum of individual utilities. If the group utilities, given a choice of zero and unit for the group, are not the sum of individual utilities,[1] according to some choice of zeros and units for each member of the group, then Pareto dominance is violated. Thus for any non-Utilitarian aggregation, there will be some Utilitarian aggregation that is better.

This does not solve the interpersonal comparison problem, because it does not tell you how to choose individual zeros and units. One choice will lead the group to rank lottery A above lottery B; another to rank B over A. In this sense, the Utilitarian Sum is still meaningless. But Harsanyi's approach did establish a kind of privileged place for taking the sum as the

---

[1] Equivalently the average. If the group is of size N we can transform the sum into an average by shrinking the units to size $\frac{1}{N}$. We are only working with groups of fixed size here.

functional form of Utilitarian aggregation. Again, without something more, almost everything philosophers have said about Utilitarianism would be meaningless.

Hopes that contemporary neurobiology would re-establish Bentham's hedonic measurement on a firm scientific foundation seem overly sanguine. Some early Utilitarian economists distinguished the concepts of pleasure and desire.[2] These appear to have different, but intertwined systems. For a while, one system was misidentified as the other. Multiple neurotransmitters are involved. Pain is something else, and neurobiology offers little prospect for combining them in the additive way that Bentham envisioned. Taking the neurobiological measurement of pleasure and pain seriously presupposes proper measurement of sensations that calibrates the measurements of neural activity and of neurotransmitter quantities. These are the problems of psychophysics all over again.

Psychophysics in the twentieth century solved some of the problems faced by psychophysics in the nineteenth. Luce's theory of semiorders (discussed in Chapter 11) shows how a system of JNDs can be represented as arising from a continuous latent variable that accounts for the "subliminal sensations." Cross-modality matching (e.g., matching the subjective brightness of a light with the loudness of a sound) does seem possible in certain domains, although the interpretation of some experimental results seems to indicate that people don't tell the difference between increments and ratios— a distinction that is crucial for quantitative meaningfulness concerns. Many of the relevant experiments have not yet been done for pleasure, and there is no guarantee that cross-modality matching for different sources of pleasure will work in the same way as those for sensations of loudness and brightness.

---

[2] For example, the nineteenth-century Utilitarian economist Arthur Marshall in the first edition of his *Principles of Economics* identified utility of a commodity with its *desirability* instead of the *satisfaction (pleasure)* brought by its consumption. This distinction between desire and satisfaction became, and continues to be, an important concept in economics.

> Thus then the desirability or utility of a thing to a person is commonly measured by the money price that he will pay for it. If at any time he is willing to pay a shilling, but no more, to obtain one gratification; and sixpence, but no more, to obtain another; then the utility of the first to him is measured by a shilling, that of the second by sixpence; and the utility of the first is exactly double that of the second.

> The only measurement with which science can directly deal is that afforded by what a person is willing to sacrifice (whether money, or some other commodity, or his own labour) in order to obtain the aggregate of pleasures anticipated from the possession of the thing itself.

> (Marshall 1890: 151)

Although the relevant mathematics for psychophysics has been substantially advanced, many empirical questions remain.

One way to move forward is to rethink the measurement of utility along different lines. Using ideas that go back to Edgeworth that are hybrid with those of Von Neumann and Morgenstern, it is possible to measure utility on a ratio scale by using preferences over episodes. This stronger scale makes meaningful Utilitarian aggregation for those episodes which have positive hedonic value for every member of the group. However, the aggregation is by product rather than sum. This is meaningful *without interpersonal comparisons*. The sum is still meaningless. Some of classical Utilitarianism survives; some does not. Some of what moral philosophers say about Utilitarianism becomes meaningful; some does not. The foregoing does not use chance at all. However, combining it with chance to get Utilitarian aggregation over lotteries over episodes can be done in different, incompatible ways. This together with Harsanyi's theorem shows that we can't get everything we might want.

A different way to advance is to keep within the Von Neumann-Morgenstern framework, but view interpersonal comparison as not being based on facts, but on convention. That raises two questions.

The first is how these conventions can be of any use. Suppose individuals somehow agree because of a convention about how to compare utilities. The nineteenth-century Utilitarian philosopher Henry Sidgwick asked why they should act to maximize the total utility of the group rather than their own personal utility. There seems no principled reason why they should, and a principled reason why they should not in cases in which the two objectives are in conflict. The answer we favor[3] requires social interaction. A group of Utilitarians can use group utility to select actions in a coordination problem. There are multiple combinations of actions that are equilibria. In these choices, individuals will be maximizing their individual utilities by maximizing the Utilitarian group utility. They will be choosing a Nash equilibrium.[4] Since everyone will be choosing it, each will be maximizing utility given what the others do. In these cases there is no conflict between the two objectives.

The second question concerns the establishment of such a convention: How does it evolve? Where coordination is important, there is a payoff for

---

[3] Due to the game theorist and philosopher Ken Binmore.

[4] A Nash equilibrium is a combination of actions such that no one can gain by unilateral deviation from that combination.

successful coordination. Given a certain amount of good will, this can drive an equilibration dynamics that can converge to agreement on the relevant aspects on interpersonal comparison. We provide general conditions on equilibration dynamics under which they will lead to such convergence. There are many possible equilibrium selection conventions that could evolve. We do not have any principled way to select one of them. We do show, however, how a Utilitarian *modus vivendi* can evolve in a small group.

Returning to the first question, the higher-order convention of Sum Utilitarianism is not the only possible way to solve coordination problems. In favorable cases, Product Utilitarians might solve coordination problems without lower level conventions of interpersonal comparison.

We go a little further than Von Neumann-Morgenstern utilities. But we do not get as far as the absolute utility numbers that some contemporary philosophers have simply postulated. There are choices to be made and alternative paths to be investigated. Implications need to be rethought. We believe that it is time for a fresh look at Utilitarianism.

PART I
THE UTILITY CONCEPT

2

Jeremy Bentham

Philosophical Radical

Jeremy Bentham's philosophy had a major impact during the late eighteenth century to early twentieth century on law, economics, and ethics. It provided an intellectual basis for nineteenth-century Utilitarianism, and played an important role in social and political reform.

Bentham's Utilitarianism was based on a simple principle of hedonism. Humans, and indeed all animals, seek pleasure and avoid pain. This is how we naturally do what is best for us. The goal of an ethical society is to maximize the overall pleasure of its members. By measuring pleasure and pain, Bentham sought to provide a rigorous scientific basis for morals.

2.1 Radical Reform

In 1823, a book entitled *Not Paul, but Jesus* appeared (see Figure 2.1). The content was so explosive that it was published under a pseudonym, Gamaliel Smith, and only part of the original text was included.[1] The real author was Jeremy Bentham. The book argues, with extensive use of Biblical text, that Christianity took the wrong path when it chose for follow Paul of Tarsus. Paul's doctrine is presented as anti-pleasure, anti-sex, and in favor of the subjugation of women to men.

Paul inveighs against bodily pleasures: "make no provision for the flesh, to gratify its desires"[2] especially sexual pleasure "it is a good thing for a man to not touch a woman."[3] He is seen opposed to any autonomy for women, "I permit no women to teach or have autonomy over men;"[4] "just as the

---

[1] The 1823 volume was to be volume I of a projected three-volume work. Additional material is now published by the Bentham project, University College London. See Bentham (2013a).

[2] Romans 13:14.

[3] 1 Corinthians 7:1.

[4] Timothy 2:11.

The Pursuit of Happiness: Philosophical and Psychological Foundations of Utility. Louis Narens and Brian Skyrms, Oxford University Press (2020). © Louis Narens and Brian Skyrms.
DOI: 10.1093/oso/9780198856450.001.0001

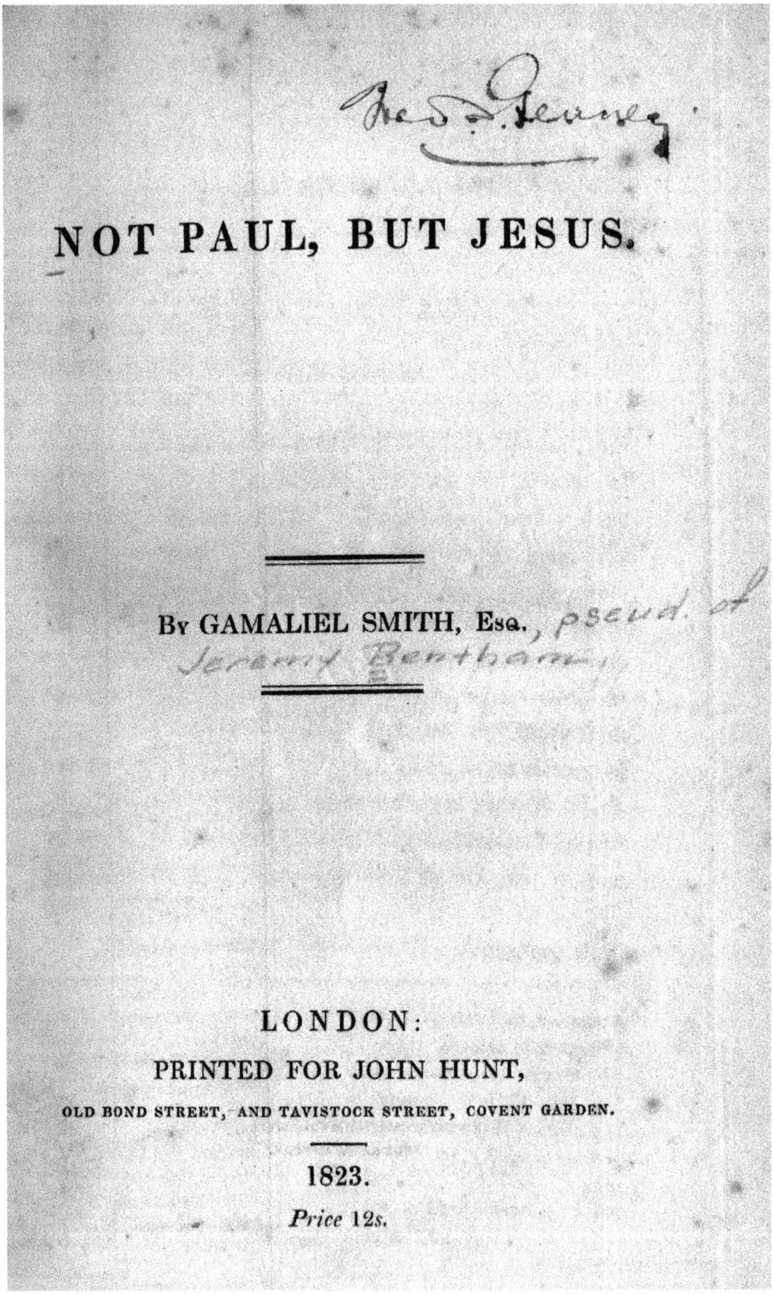

NOT PAUL, BUT JESUS.

By GAMALIEL SMITH, Esq., *pseud. of Jeremy Bentham,*

LONDON:

PRINTED FOR JOHN HUNT,

OLD BOND STREET, AND TAVISTOCK STREET, COVENT GARDEN.

1823.

Price 12s.

Figure 2.1 Thanks to Special Collections at the University of California, Irvine libraries for this scan of the title page of their copy.

Church is subject to Christ, so also let wives be subject to their husbands in all things."[5]

Bentham argues that there none of this in the teachings of Jesus.

> Not so Jesus: ... for anything that appears in any one of the four histories we have of him,—no harm did he see in anything that gives pleasure. What every man knows—and what Jesus knew as well as any man—for neither in words nor in acts did he deny it—is,—that happiness, at what time soever experienced,—happiness, to be anything, must be composed of pleasures: and, be the man who he may, of what it is that gives pleasure to him, he alone can be judge.[6]

The book ends with the statement that Paul, who warned against the Antichrist, was himself a true Antichrist.[7]

This reading of scripture served to highlight Bentham's own hedonism, which he followed wherever it led. Pleasure is good; pain is bad. Overall pleasure in society could be increased by changes is the laws of the land.

Bentham reasoned that women were as capable of feeling pleasure and pain as men. Women should not be trapped in unpleasant marriages; they should be free to divorce. This would increase their pleasure more than it would decrease, if at all, that of the husband. Women should have the right to vote.[8]

There is no reason that sex should be confined within marriage; nor that sex should only be for procreation. Bentham saw procreation as more of a problem than a goal, given the inevitable overpopulation problem foretold by Malthus. There is nothing in principle wrong with homosexuality. Sexual orientation should be a matter of personal choice, and the law should stay out of it. "It is wonderful that nobody has ever yet fancied it to be sinful to scratch where it itches."[9]

---

[5] Ephesians 5:24.

[6] Bentham (1823: 394).

[7] An even more inflammatory text, *Sextus*, written in 1817 was supposed to form part of volume III of *Not Paul, but Jesus,* but was too controversial to be published at all during Bentham's lifetime. Due to the Bentham project at University College London, it is now available, both separately and in an assembled version of volume III. See Bentham (2013a,b).

[8] For more on Bentham on women's rights, see Williford, (1975) who argues that J. S. Mill, in his famous essay of the subject (1869), was following Bentham's lead.

[9] Bentham (2013b).

Women should not be slaves to marriage, but there was a real slave trade in England. Bentham opposed black slavery on the same Utilitarian grounds. The potential gain in utility for a freed slave is greater than the potential loss to the previous master. "No one who is free is willing to become a slave; no one is a slave but he wishes to become free." But emancipation should not be so sudden as to leave the ex-slaves without means to earn a living, and worse-off than before.[10] First the slave trade should be abolished in England, then slavery in England, and gradually slavery in the rest of the world.

If black people from Africa who were traded in Liverpool were literal slaves, one could argue the inhabitants of the colonies of European nations were in a kind of slavery to their foreign masters. The same Utilitarian argument can again be made. The colonies would gain more utility by being freed than the colonizers would lose by freeing them. Bentham accordingly opposed Colonialism, against the current of history, with a steadfastness not matched by later Utilitarians.[11]

And at home, the poor were also in a kind of servitude. It was not only women who were disenfranchised, but also men who were not landowners. Food prices were kept high by the corn laws. Children worked long hours. Debtors went to prison. Petty theft was punished by hanging. It seemed obvious to Bentham and to his fellow Utilitarians that the sum total utility of society could be increased by modest reforms in these areas.

Bentham's followers—the Philosophical Radicals—continued after his death to push for some—but not all—of his projected reforms. They did not do it alone, but with allies in the clergy and elsewhere, they accomplished a lot. The corn laws were repealed in 1846, with the impetus of the Irish famine. Suffrage was extended, in a series of steps, to widening classes of men. Women had to wait until the twentieth century. In 1918 the vote was extended to selected classes of women over the age of 30. It took ten more years until all women were included.[12] Divorce was legalized in 1857. Bentham lived to see the slave trade abolished in the British Empire in 1807. The practice of slavery itself was abolished six years after his death in 1838.

---

[10] See Rosen (2005).

[11] For example, J. S. Mill (1859) "despotism is a legitimate form of government in dealing with barbarians" in his famous essay "On Liberty." See the introduction and essays in Shultz and Varouxakis (2005) especially that by Pitts (2005).

[12] New Zealand gave all women the right to vote in 1893, Australia in 1902, the United States in 1920.

2.2 Measuring Utility

Foundational questions were understandably on the back burner while changing the world. But Bentham was not unaware of them. Before one asks whether Utilitarianism is good or bad ethics, one needs to know what it means. If Utilitarianism says that the total good of society is the sum of pleasures (less pains) of its individual members, then its meaning depends on how the things to be summed are to be measured.

Bentham worried about this. First, for an individual, how are pleasures of a specified kind to be measured? Then, since there are pleasures of multiple kinds, how are they aggregated? That is, how are they put onto one scale so that the total pleasure for an individual can be meaningfully determined; likewise for pains? Then, if we have a measure of aggregate pleasure and one of aggregate pain, how are they combined to give a measure of overall hedonic value?

Supposing answers to these questions, there remains a final problem. How are individuals' hedonic values to be combined to give a meaningful Sum Utility for society? This is the problem of interpersonal comparison of utilities of which Bentham was well aware. Only when these problems are given a positive solution, if only in some coarse-grained way, can we say what Utilitarianism says is good for society.

Bentham, unlike many of his successors, recognized these problems, thought about them, and had tentative answers to some of them. Starting with the simplest question about how to measure a specific type of pleasure, he came up with the notion of JND (used later in the psychophysics of Fechner):

> the degree of intensity possessed by that pleasure which is the faintest of any that can be distinguished to be pleasure, may be represented by unity. Such a degree of intensity is in every day's experience: according as any pleasures are perceived to be more and more intense, they may be represented by higher and higher numbers.[13]

A noticeable increment is an "atom of pleasure." To measure a pleasure, you simply add up the atoms to take you from no pleasure to this pleasure.

---

[13] Bentham, in Halevy (1995 [1901]: vol. 1, p. 398).

Now consider two different kinds of pleasures, say one from food and another from listening to music. Each can be measured on its own scale, but how are they to be put on the same scale. It would have been simple enough to just postulate that an atom of one type of pleasure is equal to an atom of the other, but Bentham does not say this. He says:

> If, of two pleasures, a man, knowing what they are, would as lief enjoy one as the other, they must be reputed equal.[14]

Disposition to choose forces comparability. How different dimensions of pleasure trade off is indicated by personal preference. The comparisons are up to the agent, and may be different for different people, or for the same person at different times.

The story for measuring pains goes the same way. There are different kinds of pains. They are measured by JND, each on its own scale. Then individual preferences are used to put them on the same scale.

> If of two pains a man would as lief escape one as the other, such two pains must be reputed equal.[15]

This leaves us with the problem of combining total pleasure and total pain. Bentham believes that one simply subtracts the pains from the pleasures, but that leaves the question of aligning units of pleasure and units of pain. This is again taken to be a matter of individual preference.

> If of two sensations, a pain and a pleasure, a man would as lief enjoy the pleasure and suffer the pain, as not enjoy the first and not suffer the latter, such pleasure and pain must be reputed equal.[16]

It is conceivable that one unit of pain cancels two units of pleasure, or conversely, this depending on the individual.[17],[18] If all the foregoing can be

---

[14] Bentham in Halévy (1995 [1901]: vol. 1, appendix II, p. 306).

[15] Bentham in Halévy (1995 [1901]: vol. 1, appendix II, p. 302).

[16] Bentham in Halévy (1995 [1901]: vol. 1, appendix II, p. 302).

[17] The masochist poses a *prima facie* problem for the account, but there are various ways to save it.

[18] Current results from physiology suggest it is naive to postulate pleasure and pain being coded on a single dimension. This is discussed in Chapter 9.

consistently carried out, a given individual's hedonic value is well-defined by a combination of counting and preference.

This leaves the definition of aggregate pleasure of a group of individuals. If summing the total pleasures (or pains) of individuals is to make sense, the individual scales, gotten as above must be combined on one scale for society. This is formally much like the problem of combining different kinds of pleasures, which Bentham just solved above. But the analogous solution is not readily available. What is the tradeoff between John's pleasures and Jane's, or between John's and Fido's, according to "society's preferences"? He does not have group preferences, and indeed is trying to define what they should be. In a candid passage, Bentham admits that he is at an impasse.

> Tis vain to talk of adding quantities which after the addition will continue distinct as they were before, one man's happiness will never be another man's happiness; a gain to one man is no gain to another; one might as well pretend to add 20 apples to 20 pears, after which you had done that could not be 40 of any one thing but 20 of each just as they were before. This addibility of the happiness of different subjects, however, when considered rigorously it may appear fictitious, is a postulatum without the allowance of which all political reasoning is at a stand.[19]

Some of Bentham's followers, such as Edgeworth, also worried about these foundational questions. But a whole series of distinguished philosophers, starting with J. S. Mill, and extending to those in the present, skated over the thin ice without thinking critically about measurement.

We have in Utilitarianism a theory whose rhetorical power changed the world[20] but whose content on closer examination remains unclear. What are we to make of this? A major part of the problem was that relevant conceptual tools had not yet been developed in Bentham's time. There was no deep understanding of measurement. Psychophysics had not been explored. Psychology of pleasure and pain was underdeveloped. The relevant neurobiology did not exist at all. Theories of convention had to await developments in the theory of games.

---

[19] From Halévy (1995, [1901]: vol 3, p. 349).

[20] Or, more accurately, part the world. Much of the world has not yet implemented the reforms that the Philosophical Radicals pushed through in England. Women do not have rights. Slavery still exists.

3

Early Utilitarians

*Nature has placed mankind under the governance of two sovereign
masters, pain and pleasure. It is for them alone to point out what
we ought to do, as well as to determine what we shall do. On the
one hand the standard of right and wrong, on the other the chain
of causes and effects, are fastened to their throne. They govern us
in all we do, in all we say, in all we think: every effort we can
make to throw off our subjection, will serve but to demonstrate
and confirm it.*

(Bentham 1789: ch. 1).

Here is a quick overview of early Utilitarians, with respect to their positions
on the meaning and measurement of utility.[1] We omit those like Marshall,
who really don't add anything new to this discussion, even though they make
other contributions. A diverse collection of views rapidly develops under the
Utilitarian umbrella. Some lose the reformist zeal. Some do not worry too
much about measurement. Bentham really stands out. We think that he has
been historically undervalued.

3.1 Jeremy Bentham

Bentham aimed to lay down principles for a Science of Morals. He wanted
a science with foundations like those of physics with mathematically stated
laws relating quantified concepts. To achieve this, pleasure and pain needed
an empirical base. "Hence to know what men will do, to tell what they
should do, or to value what they have done, one must be able to measure
varying 'lots' of pleasure or pain. How are such measurements to be made?"
Bentham's basic approach to utility, that is, the measurement of pleasure-
pain, was to measure the pleasure(-pain) experience in terms of its intensity
and duration:

[1] For further reading, we recommend Ivan Moscati's excellent book, *Measuring Utility* (2018).

The Pursuit of Happiness: Philosophical and Psychological Foundations of Utility. Louis Narens and Brian Skyrms,
Oxford University Press (2020). © Louis Narens and Brian Skyrms.
DOI: 10.1093/oso/9780198856450.001.0001

The unit of intensity is the faintest sensation that can be distinguished to be pleasure or pain; the unit of duration is a moment of time. Degrees of intensity and duration are to be counted in whole numbers, as multiples of these units.

The unit of intensity multiplied by the unit of duration produced a unit of pleasure-pain, and thus the multiplication of their degrees produced a measure of pleasure-pain. Taking the sum of this pleasure-pain measure (with pains receiving negative numbers) over the duration of an episode produces a number called the *utility* for that episode. In the first analysis, an individual's utility is thus measured by just counting atoms of utility. Utility comes in discrete units. It has the structure of whole numbers, positive, negative, or zero.

The picture becomes more complicated when considering the means by which various pleasures and various pains are to be combined on a common scale of measurement. Bentham was well aware of the range of pleasures, and produced long lists of them. One of his own life-long pleasures was listening to music. Since he is measuring different kinds of pleasure in terms of just noticeable "particles" of pleasure, he could have said that all count as the same size. We have not found anywhere that he says this. Instead he uses an individual's preferences to put her pleasures and pains on one scale. The details are not worked out, but this leaves different possibilities open. Which is right for a person at a time is an empirical question.

Bentham later expanded his discussion of Utilitarian value:

Considered with reference to an individual, in every element of human happiness, in every element of its opposite unhappiness, the *elements*, or say dimensions of value (it has been seen,) are four: intensity, duration, propinquity, certainty; add, if in a political community, extent. Of these five, the first, it is true, is not susceptible of precise expression: it not being susceptible of measurement. But the four others are.[2]

Bentham still worries about measurement, but now seems to contradict his account of measurement of intensity: "Of these five, the first [intensity] is not susceptible of precise expression: it not being susceptible of measurement."

---

[2] From Bentham's *Codification Proposal* (1822: 11).

Measurement of intensity is what JND were supposed to accomplish. Bentham had different ideas at different times.

He handled the dimension of certainty as follows: The utility of an episode E happening with probability p is just p times the utility of E. This is the only risk component in his utility theory. The dimension of extent, is concerned with "the number of persons to whom [happiness] *extends*."

Propinquity is a factor that multiplies utility by a positive number the utility of an immediately experienced version of the episode. It is like a discount factor for future episodes, except it can also lead to an increase of the utility of a future episode. Bentham did not deal with the subtleties of how a future version of an episode is related to an immediately experienced one. This context effect of dependence on the past creates serious problems for modeling hedonic decision making.

Extent is handled by the Utilitarian Sum. The goal of Utilitarianism, "The greatest good for the greatest number" amounted to maximizing the sum of the utilities of a population. The population's pleasure—the sum of all the individuals' pleasures—is measured by the sum of other individuals' utilities as determined by their utility functions. We know that in private, Bentham was skeptical about interpersonal comparison of utility, and thus about whether the Utilitarian Sum was even meaningful. Recall the passage found in his unpublished manuscripts:

> Tis vain to talk of adding quantities which after the addition will continue distinct as they were before, one man's happiness will never be another man's happiness; a gain to one man is no gain to another; one might as well pretend to add 20 apples to 20 pears, after which you had done that could not be 40 of any one thing but 20 of each just as they were before. This addibility of the happiness of different subjects, however, when considered rigorously it may appear fictitious, is a postulatum without the allowance of which all political reasoning is at a stand.[3]

For practical political reform, the sum needed to be upheld, if only in some coarse-grained, approximate form. Bentham and some later Utilitarians developed a different approach to this problem: to somehow use money as a measure of individual and group utility:

[3] From Halévy (1995 [1901]: vol. 3, p. 349).

If of two pleasures a man, knowing what they are, would as lief enjoy the one as the other, they must be reputed equal. . . . If of two pains a man had as lief escape the one as the other, suc'h two pains must be reputed equal. If of two sensations, a pain and a pleasure, a man had as lief enjoy the pleasure and suffer the pain, as not enjoy the first and not suffer the latter, such pleasure and pain must be reputed *equal,* or, as we may say in this case, *equivalent.*

If then between two pleasures the one produced by the possession of money, the other not, a man had as lief enjoy the one as the other, such pleasures are to be reputed equal. But the pleasure produced by the possession of money, is as the quantity of money that produces it: money is therefore the measure of this pleasure. But the other pleasure is equal to this; the other pleasure therefore is as the money that produces this; therefore money is also the measure of that other pleasure. It is the same between pain and pain; as also between pain and pleasure.

. . . If then, speaking of the respective quantities of various pains and pleasures and agreeing in the same propositions concerning them, we would annex the same ideas to those propositions, that is, if we would understand one another, we must make use of some common measure. The only common measure the nature of things affords is money.

I beg a truce here of our man of sentiment and feeling while from necessity, and it is only from necessity, I speak and prompt mankind to speak a mercenary language. . . . Money is the instrument for measuring the quantity of pain or pleasure. Those who are not satisfied with the accuracy of this instrument must find out some other that shall be more accurate, or bid adieu to Politics and Morals.

(Quoted from Halévy 1995 [1901]: vol. I, pp. 410, 412, 414)

Bentham took money as a rough way of measuring happiness. But he could not identify quantity of utility with quantity of money. He believed in the diminishing marginal utility of money, that is, an increment of wealth at a higher wealth level will produce a smaller increase in happiness than it would at a lower level:

[The] quantity of happiness produced by a particle of wealth (each particle being of the same magnitude) will be less and less at every particle; the second will produce less than the first, the third than the second, and so on.

(Bentham 1843a: 229)

for by high dozes of the exciting matter applied to the organ, its sensibility is in a manner worn out.

(Bentham 1843b: 15)

The diminishing marginal utility of money was an important part of the Utilitarian argument for social reforms.

If Bentham had read Daniel Bernoulli, and had thought that we could take everyman's utility to be well-approximated some specific function that embodied the diminishing marginal utility of wealth, he might have pursued this line as a justification of a more egalitarian society. He does not take this step and there is no evidence that he had read Bernoulli.

Mitchell (1918) provides the following succinct summary of the legacy of Bentham's hedonic calculus.

The net resultant of all these reflections upon the felicific calculus collected from Bentham's books and papers might be put thus: (1) The intensity of feelings cannot be measured at all; (2) even in the case of a single subject, qualitatively unlike feelings cannot be compared except indirectly through their pecuniary equivalents; (3) the assumption that equal sums of money represent equal sums of pleasure is unsafe except in the case of small quantities; (4) all attempts to compare the feelings of different men involve an assumption contrary to fact. That is a critic's version of admissions wrung from Bentham's text; a disciple's version of his master's triumphs might run: (1) The felicific calculus attains a tolerable degree of precision since all the dimensions of feeling save one [i.e., intensity] can be measured; (2) the calculus can handle the most dissimilar feelings by expressing them in terms of their monetary equivalents; (3) in the cases which are important by virtue of their frequency, the pleasures produced by two sums of money are as the sums producing them; (4) taken by and large for scientific purposes men are comparable in feeling as in other respects.... Heat these two versions in the fire of controversy and one has the substantial content of much polemic since Bentham's day.

(p. 172)

3.2 John Stuart Mill

John Stuart Mill was literally a second generation Utilitarian. His father, James Mill, was Jeremy Bentham's secretary and a prominent Utilitarian in his own right. Bentham assisted James Mill is raising him. His essay, *Utilitarianism*, is perhaps the most read, and most commentated, exposition of the doctrine. J. S. Mill is widely credited with introducing qualities of pleasures into Utilitarianism whereas Bentham was supposed to hold that only quantity of pleasure was important. Thus, for instance, in 1903 G. E. Moore wrote: "It is well known that Bentham rested his case for Hedonism on 'quantity of pleasure' alone." Higher pleasures are supposed to be more important than lower pleasures for J. S. Mill, while they were supposed to count the same for Bentham.

So the story goes. Mill's discussion has been criticized, but from our perspective, we think for the wrong reasons. Here is what Mill says:

> What do you mean by difference of quality in pleasures? What, according to you, makes one pleasure more valuable than another, merely as a pleasure, if not its being greater in amount? There is only one possible answer to this.
>
> Pleasure P1 is more desirable than pleasure P2 if: all or almost all people who have had experience of both give a decided preference to P1, irrespective of any feeling that they ought to prefer it.
>
> If those who are competently acquainted with both these pleasures place P1 so far above P2 that they prefer it even when they know that a greater amount of discontent will come with it, and wouldn't give it up in exchange for any quantity of P2 that they are capable of having, we are justified in ascribing to P1 a superiority in quality that so greatly outweighs quantity as to make quantity comparatively negligible.
>
> (Utilitarianism Ch 2)

What does this mean? Some have taken Mill to be saying that pleasures are lexicographically ordered, such that any small amount of a higher pleasure, such as doing philosophy, outweighs any amount of a lower pleasure. If so, we should expect Socrates to have been a teetotaler and celibate, although the opposite seems to have been the case. Most scholars consider this position to be too ridiculous to attribute to Mill.

The last quoted clause from Mill offers some escape, "a superiority in quality that so greatly outweighs quantity as to make quantity comparatively negligible." This suggests a tradeoff between the higher pleasure on its scale with the lower pleasure on its scale to put them on the same overall pleasure scale, where the tradeoff favors the higher pleasures. Mill's talk of *quality* then comes down to saying that there are different dimensions of *quantity* and they need to be combined in one quantitative dimension. We do not see this as incompatible with Bentham. Bentham certainly was sensitive to the higher pleasures. And Bentham suggests a way to combine different dimensions of pleasure into one overall quantity. It is hard to see what Mill added other than, as Bain (1882) says, two or three pages of eloquent prose.[4]

There is another strand of Mill's thought that plays an important, though negative, role in the development of early Utilitarianism. In 1848, John Stuart Mill wrote a book on political economy that became a leading text in the field. Here he might have been expected to introduce the Utilitarian theory of value into economics. He did not make this contribution, but instead stuck with the labor theory of value, inherited from Adam Smith and David Ricardo. The introduction of utility into the economic theory of market behavior fell to William Stanley Jevons.

In the Preface to his 1871 book, *Theory of Political Economy*,[5] Jevons makes the break with tradition clear.

> The contents of the following pages can hardly meet with ready acceptance among those who regard the Science of Political Economy as having already acquired a nearly perfect form. I believe it is generally supposed that Adam Smith laid the foundations of this science; that Malthus, Anderson, and Senior added important doctrines; that Ricardo systematised the whole; and, finally, that Mr. J. S. Mill filled in the details and completely expounded this branch of knowledge. Mr. Mill appears to have had a similar notion; for he distinctly asserts that there was nothing; in the Laws of Value which remained for himself or any future writer to clear up. Doubtless it is difficult to help feeling that opinions adopted and confirmed by such eminent men have much weight of probability in their favour. Yet, in the other sciences this weight of authority has not been allowed to restrict the free examination of new opinions and theories; and it has often been ultimately proved that authority was on the wrong side.

---

[4] To make sense of the standard story, one might say that Bentham thought that one JND of a higher pleasure counts as much in computing overall quantity of pleasure as one JND of a lower pleasure, while Mill thinks that one JND of of the higher pleasure counts as many JND of a lower pleasure. The problem with this reading is that neither Mill nor Bentham says what is required. We will revisit this issue when we come to Edgeworth, who does equate JNDs.

[5] Quotations below from the 1888 edition.

3.3 William Stanley Jevons

Jevons founded exchange value of a good, not on the labor it contained, but on utility functions of agents doing the exchange. A unit of a good generally became less valuable the more you had; this is declining marginal utility of the good. Producing a good generally has increasing marginal disutility. Market equilibrium could be determined by marginal utilities. All this is spelled out mathematically by use of the differential calculus, bringing economics closer to physics. Marginal utility is just the first derivative of the utility function. These ideas were the core of what is called the *marginal revolution*. Jevons fired an opening shot in England, simultaneously with Carl Menger in Vienna and Leon Walras in Lausanne. It is clear that Bentham's discrete particles of utility are out of the picture. Utility has to be a continuous magnitude, like length, volume, or mass.

Jevons was interested in market behavior. Regarding the meaningfulness of the Utilitarian Sum total of happiness, he was publicly as skeptical as Bentham was in private.

> The reader will find, again, that there is never, in any single instance, an attempt made to compare the amount of feeling in one mind with that in another. I see no means by which such comparison can be accomplished. The susceptibility of one mind may, for what we know, be a thousand times greater than that of another. But, provided that the susceptibility was different in a like ratio in all directions, we should never be able to discover the difference. Every mind is thus inscrutable to every other mind, and no common denominator of feeling seems to be possible.
>
> (1888 [1871]: 14)

This did not bother Jevons. He wanted to make economics a science, not ethics. Utilitarian ethics is thrown out the window. Pleasure and pain stand behind the utility attached to goods, as manifest in market behavior. There should then be a way of measuring pleasure and pain, and a way of translating this quantity into the utility function used in marginal economics. However, Jevons is also a skeptic about the measuring pleasure and pain in an individual.

> I hesitate to say that men will ever have the means of measuring directly the feelings of the human heart. A unit of pleasure or of pain is difficult even to conceive; but it is the amount of these feelings which is continually

prompting us to buying and selling, borrowing and lending, labouring and resting, producing and consuming; and *it is from the quantitative effects of the feelings that we must estimate their comparative amounts.*

(p. 11)

This seems to leave Jevons' continuous, differentiable exchange utility functions without any foundation. The difficulty did not escape Jevon's critics. Consider the following from an anonymous (1871) review of Jevons (1871), that is rather pointedly quoted by Edgeworth:

We can tell that one pleasure is greater than another; but that does not help us. To apply the mathematical methods, pleasure must be in some way capable of numerical expression; we must be able to say, for example, that the pleasure of eating a beefsteak is to the pleasure of drinking a glass of beer as five to four. The words convey no particular meaning to us; and Mr. Jevons, instead of helping us, seems to shirk the question. We must remind him that, in order to fit a subject for mathematical inquiry, it is not sufficient to represent some of the quantities concerned by letters.

(Anon. 1871)

Jevons tries to defend himself against such criticisms by pointing out that indirect measurement is possible in physics. But his ideas for indirect measurement seem circular on their face. Utility functions for goods are determined by pleasures and pains, and pleasures and pains are measured by utility functions for goods. Jevons says many things, but in fact has no real answer to these questions. What he did was to postulate differentiable utility functions, and then apply the calculus to develop a theory of market behavior.

3.4 Francis Ysidro Edgeworth

Francis Ysidro Edgeworth in his 1881 *Mathematical Psychics* was a marginalist who aimed to fill the gaps in Jevons' account by using the methods of psychophysics. He was familiar with the psychophysics of Weber, Fechner, and Wundt that we will visit Chapter 4. He solves the problems of intrapersonal and interpersonal comparisons of utility at a stroke—all just noticeable differences in utility are equal. This not only provides a foundation for individual choice behavior, but also gives meaning to the Utilitarian Sum of happiness. Edgeworth does not shrink from making ethical recommendation for society on this basis.

He maintained that utility consisted of three comparable dimensions. On pages 7 and 8 he writes the following, with his footnotes enclosed within brackets:

Utility, as Professor Jevons says, has two dimensions, intensity and time. The unit in each dimension is the just perceivable [Wundt, *Physiological Psychology*] increment. The implied equation to each other of each *minimum sensible* is a first principle incapable of proof. It resembles the equation to each other of undistinguishable events or cases [Laplace, *Essai–Probabilities*, p. 7] which constitutes the first principle of the mathematical calculus of *belief.* It is doubtless a principle acquired in the course of evolution. The implied equatability of time intensity units, irrespective of distance in time and kind of pleasure, is still imperfectly evolved. Such is the unit of *economical* calculus.

For moral calculus a further dimension is required; to compare the happiness of one person with the happiness of another, and generally the happiness of groups of different members and different average happiness.

Such comparison can no longer be shirked, if there is to be any systematic morality at all. It is postulated by distributive justice. It is postulated by the population question—that horizon in which every moral prospect terminates—which is presented to the far-seeing at every turn, on the most sacred and the most trivial occasions. You cannot spend sixpence utilitarianly, without having considered whether your action tends to increase the comfort of a limited number, or numbers with limited comfort; without having compared such alternative utilities.

In virtue of what *unit* is such comparison possible? It is here submitted: Any individual experiencing a unit of pleasure-intensity during a unit of time is to "count for one." [In the Pure, for a *fraction,* in the Impure, imperfectly evolved, Utilitarianism.] Utility, then, has *three* dimensions; a mass of utility, "lot of pleasure," is greater than another when it has more *intensity-time-number* units. The third dimension is doubtless an evolutional acquisition; and is still far from perfectly evolved.

Looking back at our triple scale, we find no peculiar difficulty about the third dimension. It is an affair of census. The second dimension is an affair of clockwork; assuming that the distinction here touched, between subjective and objective measure of time, is of minor importance. But the first dimension, where we leave the safe ground of the objective, equating to unity *each minimum sensible,* presents indeed peculiar difficulties. *Atoms of pleasure* are not easy to distinguish and discern; more continuous than sand, more discrete than liquid; as it were nuclei of the just-perceivable, embedded in circumambient semi-consciousness. We cannot count the golden sands of life; we cannot number the "innumerable smiles" of seas of love; but we seem to be capable of observing that there is here a *greater,* there a *less,* multitude of pleasure-units, mass of happiness; and that is enough.

And in his 1879 *Mind* article:

AXIOM.—Pleasure is measurable, and all pleasures are commensurable; so much of one sort of pleasure felt by one sentient being equateable to so much of other sorts of pleasure felt by other sentients.

(p. 396)

He again cites the psychophysics of Wilhelm Wundt's *Principles of Physiological Psychology* in support.

From its beginning in 1860 until present, such measurement had many critics. Is the postulation of equality a moral axiom, or a matter of convention,[6] or an empirical question? The empirical research on the matter is so far is consistent with Edgeworth's view that the equality of JNDs is incapable of proof. Some, however, consider such equality an empirical matter. For example, in a review of psychophysical research Teghtsoonian (2012) writes the following about cross-modal equal JNDS:

What is being assumed is that a JND defined on one of those [physical] continua will be matched by a JND on the other. Indeed, it is an empirical question that, to my knowledge, has yet to be tested.

(p. 170)

Since Edgeworth's Axiom applies to interpersonal comparisons (which Edgeworth calls "moral calculus") as well as intrapersonal comparisons (which he calls economic calculus), we might expect his social philosophy to be highly egalitarian, like that of Bentham. Such is not the case:

---

[6] A criticism of equal sized JND by the nineteenth-century physiologist, Johannes von Kries, that still holds up today is presented in Section 4.5.

Yet in the minds of many good men among the moderns and the wisest of the ancients, there appears a deeper sentiment in favor of aristocratical privilege—the privilege of man above brute, of civilized above savage, of birth, of talent, and of the male sex.

(Edgeworth 1879: 405–6)

This is justified by differences in discrimination and, thus, counting just noticeable differences as equal, in capacity for pleasure.

He assumes the existence of individual differences in the capacity for pleasure:

An individual has greater *capacity for happiness* than another when for the same amount whatsoever of means he obtains a greater amount of pleasure, *and also* for the same increment (to the same amount) whatsoever of means a greater increment of pleasure.

(Edgeworth 1879: 395)

Capacity, however, is not weakly ordered: Person A may enjoy amount a from commodity X more than person B, but person B may enjoy a different amount b more than person A. It is however transitive. Edgeworth theorizes that people with greater capacity for happiness will tend to labor harder, because their marginal returns for a given amount diminishes less; thus those with greater capacity for happiness tend to be richer than those with lesser capacity. Since the Utilitarian imperative is to pile up the most units of pleasure for society, the rich should indeed have more goods than the poor. Likewise, he thinks that men are supposed to have more capacity for pleasure that women. He quotes the following from Tennyson:

Woman is the lesser man
and thy passions match'd with mine,
are as moonlight unto sunlight
and as water unto wine.

In the same way he explains racism and colonialism. English upper-class white males are supposed to have more JND and thus should get more goods.

He stops short of categorically endorsing these suppositions. As Edgeworth notes, these judgments are empirical. They are open to refutation by future psychophysics. If future measurement of atoms of pleasure should show women to have a capacity equal to that of men, of Irish to be equal to

English, of Untouchables to be equal to Brahmins, these judgements would stand refuted. Edgeworth might be shocked to see that today the wine critic for the *Financial Times* is a woman.

There is a tension, indeed an equivocation, in Edgeworth's discussion of the "golden sands of life." Are they finite atoms that can be counted, at least in principle, for the Utilitarian Sum of happiness, or infinitesimals, as used intuitively in the calculus? He moves back and forth between both.

When doing economics, Edgeworth treats utility of a good as a continuous, function of the quantity of that good, and is comfortable using the first and second derivatives of that function:

> The rate of increase of pleasure decreases as its means increase. The postulate asserts that the second differential of pleasure with regard to means is continually negative. It does not assert that the first differential is continually positive. It is supposable (though not probable) that means increased beyond a certain point increase only pain.
>
> (Edgeworth 1979: 397)

We will see in Chapter 4 that the final sentence is again a reference to Wundt's psychophysics of pleasure.

Edgeworth uses this machinery of the calculus to create a theory of indifference curves. An indifference curve between two goods shows different combinations of goods with the same utility. Diminishing marginal utility tells us something about the shape of the curves. They allow an analysis of market behavior. As we will see in Chapter 5, a later generation of economists reinterpreted Edgeworth's theory in terms of a thinner conception of utility. But at this point in its development, Utilitarianism sees its foundations as being in psychology, and specifically in psychophysics. We turn to early psychophysics in Chapter 4.

4

Nineteenth-Century Psychophysics

Psychophysics was born in the nineteenth-century with investigations of Ernst Weber, Wilhelm Fechner, and Wilhelm Wundt. They succeeded one another in that order, at the University of Leipzig. Weber was a physiologist; Fechner initially a physicist; Wundt a philosopher and psychologist. The discipline of psychophysics was aimed at discovering quantitative laws linking the psychological and physical realms. In particular, laws were meant to connect physical intensities of stimulus to the resulting psychological intensities of sensation. Utilitarians, such as Edgeworth, saw a direct application of this conceptual framework and its methodology to Utility.

4.1 Weber, Fechner, and Just Noticeable Differences

Weber conducted experiments on perception of weight, temperature, and pressure. The unit by which sensations were measured were JND, as Bentham had proposed. Fechner, inspired by Weber's work, developed psychophysics as a discipline. He invented the name and wrote a massive two-volume work laying out the field. Fechner had philosophical motivations. He believed that mind and matter were common aspects of one underlying reality, a view with close connections to that of Spinoza. *External psychophysics,* in his terminology, was to examine the effect of external stimuli on sensation. *Internal psychophysics* was to examine the relation of sensations to states of the brain. Volume 1 of his work dealt with external psychophysics—our concern here—volume 2 with internal psychophysics. Fechner did not have enough neurobiology for volume 2 to amount to much, but we today have more with extensive continuing developments. We will look at some things that are known about neurobiology of pleasure in Part II of this book. Fechner, like Bentham, had a view of pleasure and pain as driving action. In 1848 he published an essay on the Pleasure Principle (*Lustprintzp*) that influenced Sigmund Freud and other prominent thinkers of the early twentieth century.

The Pursuit of Happiness: Philosophical and Psychological Foundations of Utility. Louis Narens and Brian Skyrms, Oxford University Press (2020). © Louis Narens and Brian Skyrms.
DOI: 10.1093/oso/9780198856450.001.0001

Fechner's external psychophysics was founded on a measurement theory using the same basic idea as Bentham of smallest perceivable stimulus. The simplest psychophysical stimuli and the easiest to experiment on were physical intensities. Much of early psychophysics focused on the following question: How is the perceived subjective intensity $\psi(x)$ of a physical stimulus x related to its physical measurement $\phi(x)$? Psychophysics assumed that there was a function F relating the two. Formally, F is said to be a *psychophysical function on the domain X* if and only if for each physical measurement of $\phi(x)$ for x in X, there is a subjective intensity measurement $\psi(x)$ such that

$$\psi(x) = F[\phi(x)].$$

Characterization of F produces what is known as a *psychophysical law.*

Are individual judgments about JND reproducible? The facts are not so simple. So an issue with this as a scientific definition is how to define and collect data about "barely perceivably more intense." The route that nineteenth-century psychologists took was to present a subject with two stimuli on the same sensory dimension and ask her to choose the one that was subjectively more intense. For example, for the dimension of physical intensities of lights of a particular wavelength, this amounted to asking the subject to choose the brighter of two lights. The subject was required to make a choice, even if she could not "perceive any difference in them"; that is, even if she has to do it by guessing. The trick for experimental psychology was to present the two stimuli x and y many times and record the number of times y was chosen over x. If y was chosen at least 75 percent of the time, then y was said to be *1 JND above x*, or "*y is 1 JND more intense x.*" This use of a probability in the definition of JND converts Bentham's scientifically vague concept into a straightforward scientific one, allowing for statistical testing and concepts of error. Each dimension was assumed to have an item z of 0 physical intensity. An item a that was 1 JND above z was said to be at *absolute threshold*. Note that Bentham's "a barely perceptual pleasure" is a similar but different concept. His concept is *phenomenological*. It is about a single item in consciousness. Absolute threshold, as defined here, is *behavioral*. It is about a particular percentage of "Yes" responses about a repeatedly presented item.

In his famous work *Elemente der Psychophysik* (Fechner 1860), *Elemente* for short, which today is considered as the foundational publication for the creation of the fields of experimental psychology and psychophysics, Fechner concluded that F had to be a logarithmic function. In the literature, $F = \log$

is usually called the *Weber-Fechner Law*. We will just call it *Fechner's Law*. Unlike the impression one is likely to get from introduction to psychology textbooks, various philosophical discussions involving JNDs and Fechner's Law, and even textbooks on psychophysics, Fechner's derivations of his Law did not use JNDs or assume results of Weber.[1] This section uses Fechner's theory of subjective intensity as it appeared in chapter 17 of his *Elemente*. In *Elemente*, Fechner uses this theory to derive his law from theoretical assumptions about subjective differences. This derivation is consistent with the methods employed in modern psychophysics.[2] Later, he cites Weber's investigations as providing empirical support for this law. Utilitarians saw Weber and Fechner as providing indirect support for their doctrine of diminishing marginal utility of goods.

4.2 Bernoulli's Utility Law

A logarithmic law relating money to utility appeared prior to Fechner in the 1731 work of the mathematician Daniel Bernoulli. In formulating his law, Bernoulli developed a concept of "utility" that was different from Bentham's. His main aim was to use his law to solve a probability puzzle proposed by his cousin the mathematician Nikolaus Bernoulli. Bernoulli's Law was apparently known by Fechner prior to his own discovery of his psychophysical law.[3]

The scientific study of determining the expected values of games of chance started with the mathematicians Fermat and Pascal around 1650. It quickly became extended to determining value of all sorts of monetary dominated prospects. In 1713, Nikolaus Bernoulli challenged the foundations of this emerging field by proposing a problem that today is known as the *St Petersburg Paradox*. It concerns the following prospect.

---

[1] For a discussion of this misrepresentation of Fechner's ideas, see page 2 of Colonius and Dzhafarov (2011).

[2] We provide a technical discussion in Appendix 4.1.

[3] Baird and Noma (1978: 15) write,

> We see that Fechner had little hope of measuring M [brain activity] and W [sensation] directly, and therefore the mapping between them was similarly out of scientific reach. How, then, did he decide upon a particular mapping. We can never know the actual conditions leading to the the proposed [log] mapping. We do know, however, that he [Fechner] was familiar with the work of the mathematicians Bernoulli, Laplace, and Poisson, who proposed that the utility of an increase in personal wealth was a function of the amount one already had.

A player may flip a fair coin until heads appears. If this is on the first flip, then the player is paid 2 ducats; if on the second flip, then paid 4 ducats; if on the third flip, 8 ducats; if on the fourth flip, 16 ducats, and so on. What would a player pay to play this game? Its expected value is,

$$2 \cdot \frac{1}{2} + 4 \cdot \frac{1}{4} + 8 \cdot \frac{1}{8} + \ldots = \infty.$$

Looking at a particular value gives a clue: If a player paid 100 ducats and heads came up in the first six flips, then the player would still be at a loss. Most players wouldn't like this kind of risk. Being in a situation like this where there is an infinite expected value but be willing to pay only a small amount to play, is called the St Petersburg Paradox. Daniel Bernoulli's solution to the paradox was to distinguish between (monetary) value and utility:

> Somehow a very poor fellow obtains a lottery ticket that will yield with equal probability either nothing or twenty thousand ducats. Will this man evaluate his chance of winning at ten thousand ducats? Would he not be ill-advised to sell this lottery ticket for nine thousand ducats? To me it seems that the answer is in the negative. On the other hand I am inclined to believe that a rich man would be ill-advised to refuse to buy the lottery ticket for nine thousand ducats. If I am not wrong then it seems clear that all men cannot use the same rule to evaluate the gamble.... But anyone who considers the problem with perspicacity and interest will ascertain that the concept of value which we have used in this rule may be defined in a way which renders the entire procedure universally acceptable without reservation. To do this the determination of the value of an item must not be based on its price, but rather on the utility it yields. The price of the item is dependent only on the thing itself and is equal for everyone; the utility, however, is dependent on the particular circumstances of the person making the estimate. Thus there is no doubt that a gain of one thousand ducats is more significant to a pauper than to a rich man though both gain the same amount.
>
> (Bernoulli 1954: 24)

With these ideas there are many utility functions of money that provide solutions to the St Petersburg Paradox. For example, prior to Daniel Bernoulli's paper—and apparently unknown to him while he was working out his theory—Gabriel Cramer suggested using the square root of ducats as a utility function for solving the paradox. Cramer's reason was similar to Bernoulli's: In a 1728 letter to Nicolas, Cramer writes,

> You ask for an explanation of the discrepancy between the mathematical calculation and the vulgar evaluation ... in their theory, mathematicians evaluate money in proportion to its quantity while, in practice, people with common sense evaluate money in proportion to the utility they can obtain from it.

Bernoulli thought that the logarithm was the natural choice because, "it is highly probable that any increase in wealth, no matter how insignificant, will always result in an increase in utility which is inversely proportionate to the quantity of goods already possessed." From this he shows it follows that utility of a quantity of ducats is a logarithm of that quantity. A proof is given in Appendix 4.2.

By a "quantity of goods," he means "to connote food, clothing, all things which add to the conveniences of life, and even to luxury—anything that can contribute to the adequate satisfaction of any sort of want." By a mathematical argument he shows that his inverse proportionality rule relates utility and wealth by the following:

$$utility = \log(wealth)$$

By both Cramer's and Bernoulli's proposals, the value of the game is finite. The value of game depends on the initial wealth of the player. In the relevant range, the two suggested Utility functions are qualitatively similar. Utility increases with wealth, but with more and more wealth, it increases ever more slowly.

4.3 Wundt on Psychophysics of Pleasure

Weber and Fechner studied the psychophysics of many sensations, but not the sensations of pleasures. Wundt, third in the lineage of psychophysicists at Leipzig, did. One might expect the shape of Weber-Fechner psychophysical law might generalize to pleasure; that pleasure would continue to increase, but increase ever more slowly, in response to increased stimulus intensity. Wundt (1874) however found a different kind of psychophysical function. Very low levels of sensory stimulation of a pleasant stimulus produced no increase in pleasantness. Beyond a point, however, further increases in sensory stimulus produced increases in perceived pleasantness, until a maximum pleasure was reached. Further increases beyond the intensity that produced maximum pleasure led to monotonic declines in perceived pleasure, all the way down to yielding increasingly painful experiences. This resulted an inverted U-shaped pattern for pleasure stimulus intensity. Today, this type of pattern is called the *Wundt Curve*.

Although Wundt's inverted U-shaped pleasure function conflicts with the kind of shape given by the log or power law psychophysical functions, it fits perfectly well into Utilitarian theory, as Edgeworth noted. It obeys the Law of Diminishing Returns, and indeed accentuates its consequences. If there is a point beyond which increasing the quantity of physical stimulus actually decreases pleasure, and if there are a limited number of relevant stimuli, then there is even less justification for great inequalities of wealth.

4.4 Plateau's Power Law

The Belgian physicist Joseph Plateau (1872) presented a mathematical argument and preliminary data. His method of derivation and experimental approach were general and applied to other psychophysical situations. It was based on using a functional equation to capture an invariance that was inherent in many psychophysical settings. While Fechner's functional equation expresses a constant relationship between physical ratios and psychological differences, Plateau's expresses a constant relationship between physical ratios and psychological ratios. Plateau (1872) writes,

> Fechner's formula leads to this consequence that, when the overall illumination increases, the differences in sensation remain constant; it seemed to me more rational, in order to explain the invariance of the general effect of the picture, to postulate *a priori* the constancy of the ratios and not the differences of the sensations.
>
> (pp. 382–3; and trans. in Falmagne 1985: 318; emphasis added)

Pleateau's experimental task consisted of providing eight artists with two disks—one painted black and the other white—with the instruction to paint a gray disk midway between them. This is a direct measurement task, because the subjects had to produce a stimulus that was *subjectively* half way between two other stimuli in terms of grayness. The eight midway disks returned to Plateau were almost identical, despite presumed illumination differences under which they were painted. Plateau assumed that each artist mixed his paint so that the ratio of the subjective intensity of white to the painted gray equaled the subjective intensity of painted gray to black. Consider the black and white disks as extreme examples of gray ones and assume a similar result would hold for any pair of gray disks A and Z of gray disks presented for judgment. Then the equation

$$\frac{\psi(A)}{\psi(M)} = \frac{\psi(M)}{\psi(Z)}$$

results, where where M is the midway disk painted by the artist and ψ is the function that measures the artist's subjective intensity of grayness. It is a known physical fact that the *ratios* of the usual physical measurements ϕ of the light for such disks do not vary with illumination. Because of this, Plateau reasoned that such ratios would be the same in each artist's studio. Combining this with his experimental results, Plateau concluded that the following law held for all gray disks A and Z,

Preserved Midway Ratio Law: $\quad \dfrac{\phi(A)}{\phi(M)} = \dfrac{\phi(M)}{\phi(Z)}$ iff $\dfrac{\psi(A)}{\psi(M)} = \dfrac{\psi(M)}{\psi(Z)}$,   4.1

where M is the gray disk produced midway between A and Z, ϕ measures the physical intensity of grays, and ψ measures subjective grayness. The functional equation solution to Equation 4.1 is the *Psychophysical Power Law,*

$$\psi = r\phi^s$$

for some positive r and s. Cramer's alternative to Bernoulli for the utility on money is a special case. In the twentieth century, the psychologist S. S. Stevens was to again propose a power law as the general psychophysical law.

Because it was based on direct measurement, simply asking subjects to produce the mid-point, Fechner did not accept Plateau's Power Law. He thought such an approach to measurement was unscientific. Plateau's measurement procedure had little impact on nineteenth-century psychophysics and utility theory. In the mid-twentieth-century psychophysics, new direct methods for obtaining psychophysical laws were promoted. This led to a debate as to which described human psychophysical subjective intensities better, Fechner's Law or the Power Law. The debate continues still today. Stevens theory of measurement is discussed in Section 10.3 and the Power Law in Section 4.4.

4.5 Von Kries

The nineteenth-century physiological psychologist Johannes Adolf von Kries raised a number of objections to Fechner's approach to JND measurement and his psychophysical law. The objection most relevant for later parts of this book are his concerns about Fechner's method depending on a convention. This is made explicit in the following quotation from Von Kries (1995 [1882]):

From these considerations it follows that the whole debate over laws of correlation between sensations and stimuli is a totally senseless debate. We can *fix a convention* such that all just-noticeable increments in sensation from a single series of intensities are to be considered equal. Having done so, we can represent a number of observed facts in what we attribute to sensation an increment proportional to the logarithm of the stimuli. But this law means nothing at all *without* that convention, as we have seen. And *with the convention* this law means nothing but the observed facts. We can just as well establish the convention that those increments in sensation should be considered equal which correspond to equal increments in stimulation. Then we can represent the same set of facts that the stronger a sensation, the greater the just-noticeable difference. One schema is no more accurate than the other. The only difference between them is a question of usefulness. It is blatantly obvious how this puts our position in stark contrast to the received reading. For Fechner and for everyone else (Note 2)[4] who has worked in his tradition since, the problem has been one of discovering '*the correct standard of measure*' for the intensity of sensation. What does that mean? The very *task* of measuring spatial magnitudes presupposes

---

[4] Note 2:

Zeller's (1881) recent article is also directed against the performance of actual measurements. It leaves unmentioned what I must take to be the core of the whole matter. When Zeller (1881, p. 9) says 'that psychological processes are not measurable in the same sense as magnitudes of space and time, because they have no invariant standard of measure . . .', then it is evident he considers a situation similar to that which would hold for space if there were no rigid bodies. To this one might justifiably counter that in the domain of sensations we could produce at least close or approximate values that might serve as such 'invariant standards of measurement'. Nor am I ready to concede that psychological processes may be unmeasurable because appearances in consciousness can only ever be compared with appearances in consciousness. No form of measurement does anything else, but to establish the relations of like with like. So we measure space only by space, and time only by time. Compare Wundt's (1883, pp. 253–254) comments on the subject, which I endorse wholeheartedly.

that one has a clear idea what it should mean that spatial magnitudes may be congruent. Yet the execution of *specific* operations of measurement is tied to the existence of bodies which have the property that they can move freely in space without change of form. At least these operations depend on the property in this much: they are enormously facilitated by it, and perhaps without such bodies these operations would be impossible. Let us imagine there were only a very few such bodies. Clearly then our execution of operations of measurement in space would depend on our ability to recognized and use those few bodies. Whoever had discovered the first of these bodies would be justified in saying: until now we could not have measured spatial extent, for want of an appropriate standard; now we have found the standard which permits us to do so. This is the sense in which Fechner thought he had revealed the just-noticeable difference as the 'true' standard of measure for the intensity of sensation. In contrast, our discussion has shown that we are really dealing with an arbitrary convention about relations of magnitudes—which can be expedient or inexpedient, but which cannot be right or wrong.

(trans. K. K. Niall; Niall, 1995: 292–3)

We agree with Von Kries that the equality of JNDs is based on a convention of measurement and is not a fact about the world. The empirical facts may be given a representation based on the convention of equal JNDs, but they may also be given alternative representations based on alternative conventions that make JNDs unequal. This is made clear in the modern Representational Theory of Measurement, which we discuss in Section 11.7. Within the Representational Theory, the measurement of fundamental physical attributes such as length, time, and mass also have such a conventional aspect.[5]

---

[5] This is because of the qualitative axiomatizations of JND structures described in section 11.2 of Luce (1956) and Narens (1994). They have algebraic characterizations at the same level as the physical measurement of length, and their individual units (e.g., a unit of one JND) can be "freely moved about" a quality through their individual transformation groups. Space and time discussed in the quotation and its footnote are not needed for such "free movements," even for the measurement of physical qualities. These are formally captured by actions of the transformation groups on the ordered qualities.

4.6 Peirce and Jastrow

In 1884, the American philosopher Charles Sanders Peirce and his student Joseph Jastrow, who went on to become a distinguished experimental psychologist,[6] performed psychophysical experiments on the perception of pressure at Johns Hopkins University. The results, published the following year in the *Proceedings of the National Academy of Sciences*, showed that, in a sense, the notion of a JND (*Unterschiedsschwelle*) as found in Fechner, does not exist:

> The tables show that the numbers of errors follow, as far as we can conveniently trace them, the numbers assigned by the probability curve,[7] and therefore destroy all presumption in favor of an Unterschiedsschwelle. The introduction and retention of this false notion can only confuse thought, while the conception of the mathematician must exercise a favorable influence on psychological experimentation.

It must have struck our reader that using .75 probability to define a JND is arbitrary. Using .6 would define a smaller difference. And so, in theory would .51. Fechner saw this, and saw a strict JND, as we shall call it, as one in which the subject would report a stimulus increment as having a greater effect more than half the time. He believed that there would be a threshold below which an increment in physical stimulus would produce no deviation at all from 50/50 psychological responses.

Peirce and Jastrow advanced the hypothesis that differences in perception vary smoothly with differences in stimulus, with zero difference in perception occurring only at zero difference in stimulus. The probabilistic nature of expressed judgments was the result of noise in the system, distributed according to the usual error law. To test this hypothesis, they required a subject who reported zero difference between two stimuli to guess which is the greater. Probability of guessing that a stimulus was higher tracked the amount that it was indeed higher, even when subjects did not a report a difference but only "guessed." The 50/50 probability that would indicate a strict JND for Fechner occurred only with equality of physical stimulus.

---

[6] One of Jastrow's later interests was the psychology of the illusions used by professional magicians. We recommend "The Psychology of Deception" (1888) and "Psychological Notes on Slight of Hand Experiments" (1896), both available online. He is also the originator of the Duck-Rabbit illusion.

They concluded that non-zero strict JNDs simply do not exist. Some kind of perception below the level of consciousness was operating. This sort of subliminal experience became a focus of Jastrow's subsequent research. If we translate this to Utilitarianism, it seems to call for subliminal pleasures and pains. Psychophysics had now moved quite a distance from Bentham's "atoms of pleasure."[7]

4.7 Conclusion

When we reach Edgeworth, Utilitarians know about psychophysics and see it as a foundation for social and economic policy. They plausibly saw determination of the shape of utility functions as relevant to determining which social institutions tend to maximize the total utility of citizens. Psychophysics, however, presupposes an answer to the problem of how to measure subjective intensity rather than providing one. For the most part, nineteenth-century psychology solved this problem in just the way that Bentham had suggested, by using just noticeable differences. Actually applying the technique uncovered difficulties, prompted refinements, led to criticism, and opened the way for more sophisticated approaches of the subsequent century. JNDs turn out to have a statistical character, rather than an absolute one. Questions are raised about the postulation of the equality of these JNDs, even for one person on one dimension. Subliminal sensations of pleasure and pain as latent variables seem hard to avoid.[8] Does psychophysics help with interpersonal comparisons? The pleasure I get from cream in my

---

[7] Contemporary psychophysics has moved even further. Fechner's Law has been generalized to the following, where stimulus b is of greater physical intensity of a:

$$\text{General Psychophysical Law: } \mathbb{P}_{a,b} = F[\psi(\phi(b)) - \psi(\phi(a))],$$

where $\mathbb{P}_{a,b}$ is the probability that b judged more intense than a, $\phi(x)$ measures x physically, $\psi(\phi(x))$ is the psychological intensity of x, and F is a function relating the difference of the psychological intensities $\psi(\phi(b)) - \psi(\phi(a))$ to $\mathbb{P}_{a,b}$. In gathering data, $\mathbb{P}$ and ϕ are observable. The problem then is to provide a theory and methodology that allow F and ψ to be estimated from data up to appropriate scale transformations. There are many theories and methodologies for accomplishing this (e.g., see Thurstone 1927; Falmagne 1985; Suppes et al. 1990: ch. 17). What they have in common is that they make assumptions about how the distribution of the observed values of $\psi(\phi(a))$ for repeated presentations of $\phi(a)$ and the distribution of the observed values of $\psi(\phi(b))$ for repeated presentations of $\phi(b)$ are related.

[8] In the twentieth century, generalizations with more scientific rigor and wider applicability became available (e.g., Thurstone's Law of Comparative Judgment, Luce's Choice Axiom, Signal Detection Theory) and became competitors. From its inception until now, Fechner's psychophysical theory, methodology, and the ideas behind them attracted much praise and criticism. This was anticipated by Fechner. He wrote,

coffee and the pleasure that you get from milk in your tea may both follow Wundt Curves, but this does nothing to put both pleasures on a common scale.

Appendix 4.1. Fechner's Law

Fechner's psychophysics concerns the relationships between the physical environment N, brain activity produced by environmental stimulation, M, and the sensation (conscious perception) W that accompanied N and M. Baird and Noma (1978) write,

> Of the three possible pairings, the mapping between brain activity and conscious sensation was the most critical. Fechner termed the theoretical study of this relationship "inner psychophysics." Unfortunately, as so often happens in science, this most crucial relationship proved to be inaccessible to direct observation. Therefore, one could only speculate about the exact properties of inner psychophysics, and this created a seemingly insurmountable barrier. To avoid this barrier, Fechner hypothesized that measured brain and subjective perception were simply alternative ways of viewing the same phenomena. One realm of the universe did not *depend* on the other in a cause-and-effect fashion; rather, they accompanied each other and were complementary in the information conveyed about the universe.
>
> (p. 12)

in his search for a mathematical relationship between M and W, Fechner assumed that sensation could be measured (theoretically) and properly located along an internal scale. The function relating values of physical and psychic magnitude represents the psychophysical transformation. The general form of this transformation was thought to be the same for all physical attributes (lights, sounds, lengths, smells). In effect, the idea was that conscious experience is *unitary*, can be ordered along an intensity scale, and bears a constant relation (except for changes in stimulus parameters) to both internal brain processes and external conditions giving rise to those processes. Hence a pluralistic, materialistic environment is mapped into a

The Tower of Babel was never finished because the workers could not reach an understanding on how they should build it; my psychophysical edifice will stand because the workers will never agree on how to tear it down. (Fechner 1887: 215)

unitary scale of conscious sensation. Although some mechanism must also be provided in this scheme for recognizing qualitative differences among attributes, this difficulty did not receive much attention from Fechner and consequently played no role in his further development of a quantitative mapping between M and W.

(p. 14)

Although the relation between the internal events M and W was the object of attention, it was clear that this relation could not be verified by direct measurement. Therefore, an alternative approach was necessary. It was possible, of course, to obtain a direct measure of N, the environmental stimulus. This, then, was a starting point, although there was no hope of measuring the brain processes triggered by N. That left W. If some measure of W were possible, however indirect, the relation between N and W could probably be determined. Fechner called the experimental quest for this relation "outer psychophysics."

(p. 17)

There are several approaches for deriving Fechner's Law. We will follow a modern reconstruction by Dzhafarov and Colonius 2011 of an approach by Fechner in volume 2 of *Elemente*. Volume 2 has not been translated into English, and many of its ideas has been ignored in the English literature. The basic idea of the reconstruction is to define a function F and a ternary relation δ on the physical measurements of N in a manner such that F maps each physical measurement $\phi(x)$ onto the sensory impression $\psi(x)$ of x, and $\delta[\phi(y), \phi(x)]$ maps the ratio of physical measurements $\dfrac{\phi(y)}{\phi(x)}$ onto the difference $\psi(y) - \psi(x)$ of the measurements $\psi(y)$ and $\psi(x)$ of the sensory impressions of x and y. A rule, called the W-Principle relating F and δ then gives Fechner's Law.

The reconstruction begins with defining for a physical dimension its *absolute threshold* as the lowest level of the physical stimulus that is detectable by the subject. The absolute threshold is denoted by the symbol o. It is the same as the concept of absolute threshold defined previously. The concept of *difference sensation* is formulated in volume 2 of *Elemente*. Dzhafarov and Colonius 2011 define it as follows:

The sensation of difference between two stimuli is the same as the increment in sensation magnitude from the lesser to the greater of the two stimuli (cf. *Elemente*, p. 85 of vol. 2).

(p. 3)

This difference, δ, is assumed by Fechner to have the following four properties for the physical measurements $\phi(a)$, $\phi(b)$, and $\phi(c)$ of the physical stimuli a, b, c such that $\phi(a) \leq \phi(b) \leq \phi(c)$:

(1) $\delta[\phi(a), \phi(b)] = 0$ iff $\phi(a) = \phi(b)$.
(2) $\delta[\phi(a), \phi(b)] = \delta[\phi(b), \phi(a)]$.
(3) $\delta[\phi(a), \phi(c)] = \delta[\phi(a), \phi(b)] + \delta[\phi(b), \phi(c)]$.
(4) The W-Principle, defined below.

Dzhafarov and Colonius, (2011: p. 4), says the following about (3): "This additivity property is central for Fechner's theory, as he repeatedly states when discussing the notion of measurement (e.g., *Elemente*, pp. 56, 60 of vol. 1, and Chapter 20 in vol. 2)."

W-Principle: There exists a non-negative function F such that for all physical measurements $\phi(o) \leq \phi(a) \leq \phi(b)$ from a dimension,

$$\delta[\phi(a), \phi(b)] = F\left(\frac{\phi(a)}{\phi(b)}\right). \qquad 4.2$$

Equation 4.2 together with

$$\delta[\phi(a), \phi(c)] = \delta[\phi(a), \phi(b)] + \delta[\phi(b), \phi(c)]$$

yields the functional equation,

$$F\left(\frac{\phi(b)}{\phi(a)}\right) + F\left(\frac{\phi(c)}{\phi(b)}\right) = F\left(\frac{\phi(c)}{\phi(a)}\right). \qquad 4.3$$

By well-known techniques involving functional equations that were available to Fechner, the solutions to Equation 4.3 yield non-negative F and positive k such that

$$\textit{Fechner's Law: } F(x) = k \log(x), \text{ for } 1 \leq x. \qquad 4.4$$

Then Equations 4.2 and 4.3 yield,

$$\textit{Fechner's difference formula: } \delta[\phi(a), \phi(b)] = k \log\left(\frac{\phi(b)}{\phi(a)}\right). \qquad 4.5$$

(1) to (4) above are theoretical assumptions about properties of the psychophysical function. Fechner's Law, Equation 4.4, is a conclusion drawn from these properties. Although theoretical and about subjective phenomena, it is refutable. In particular a famous empirically derived law of Fechner's teacher, the physiologist Ernst Weber (1840), Weber's Law, is a consequence of Fechner's Law applied to Weber's empirical setting, and thus the holding Weber's Law provides empirical support for Fechner's theory.

Weber's Law is about JND: It says that there exists a non-negative function F and a positive constant c such that for all physical measurements ϕ on a dimension, if $\phi(o) \leq \phi(a) < \phi(b)$, where o is absolute threshold and b is just-noticeably different from a, that is, b is 1 JND from a, then

$$\text{Weber's Law:} \quad \frac{\phi(b)}{\phi(a)} = 1 + c, \qquad\qquad 4.6$$

where c is *Weber's constant* given by the formula,

$$\frac{\phi(b) - \phi(a)}{\phi(b)} = c.$$

The proof is as follows: Assume Fechner's difference formula and Weber's Law. Then, on the sensation difference measurement representation δ, it follows from Equation 4.5 that the difference of 1 JND has constant value $k \log(1 + c)$ *everywhere on the δ representation.*

The following is a useful general definition of representing a dimension by JNDs: We say that a function θ on the reals is a *JND representation of size* d if and only if there exists a positive real number d such that for all a on the dimension of stimuli,

$$\theta[\phi(a)] - \phi(a) = d.$$

In this case, d is said to be "1 JND."

The foregoing showed that Fechner's difference formula and Weber's Law implied a JND representation of size $k \log(1 + c)$, where c is Weber's constant and k is a positive real. However, a JND representation for a situation satisfying Weber's Law is not sufficient for having the Fechner difference formula hold.[9]

---

[9] Representations other than θ having exactly the same JND structure as θ can be constructed from θ as follows: Let g be any strictly monotonic function from absolute threshold $\phi(o)$

Appendix 4.2. Comparison of Fechner's and Bernoulli's Approaches

Both Bernoulli and Fechner derive logarithmic laws from phenomena that have similar underlying mathematical structure. The derivation of Bernoulli used the idea that the utility u for each small increment $d(W)$ of wealth from the amount of W was constantly proportional to W. The is reminiscent of Weber's Law, but is different from it, because $d(x)$ exists for all small x. The proportionality rule gives rise to the *differential equation,*

$$\frac{du}{dx} = \frac{r}{W(x)}, \qquad\qquad 4.7$$

r a positive constant. The solution to Equation 4.7 is

$$u = \text{a logarithmic function.}$$

The reconstruction of Fechner presented above used the *functional equation,*

$$F\left(\frac{\phi(b)}{\phi(a)}\right) + F\left(\frac{\phi(c)}{\phi(b)}\right) = F\left(\frac{\phi(c)}{\phi(a)}\right), \qquad\qquad 4.8$$

to derive that F was a logarithmic function. Differential and functional equations play an important role in behavioral science. Differential equations have more of a role in economics than in psychophysics. They are useful for formulating mathematical theory, but less so in the design of experiments. They are not directly testable because such tests would require comparing stimuli that are arbitrary close to one another, and "arbitrary close" is not empirically achievable. Functional equations can lead to direct empirical tests.

As mentioned previously, Fechner had another derivation of his law. This derivation is based on a differential equation that had the same mathematical form as Bernoulli's, as presented in Equation 4.7. He arrived at this by going from small differences to differentials. Luce and Edwards (1958) write,

---

to $\Theta[\phi(o)]$ such that $g[\phi(o)] = \phi(o)$, $g(\Theta[\phi(o)]) = \Theta[\phi(o)]$, and for x in the interval $(\phi[o], \Theta[\phi(o)])$, $g(x) \neq x$. For each integer n, if y is in the interval $[n \cdot \phi(o), n \cdot \Theta(\phi(o))]$, let $\sigma(y) = ng(x)$, where $x - n$ is in the interval $[\phi(o), \Theta[\phi(o)]]$. Then σ is another JND representation that is different from Θ but agrees everywhere with Θ on JND differences.

How did Fechner make this step from differences (deltas) to differentials? He used what he called a "mathematical auxiliary principle," the essence of which is that what is true for differences as small as jnd's ought also to be true for all smaller differences and so true in the limit as they approach zero (differentials). If this argument were acceptable (which it is not), the rest would be simple. Equation [Equation 4.7], when integrated, yields the familiar logarithmic relationship between sensation and stimulus which is known as Fechner's law.

(p. 225)

Fechner's Law plus Weber's Law implies a JND representation of size $log(1 + c)$, where c is Weber's constant. Thus Fechner's Law plus Weber's Law implies a representation in which all JNDs are the same size. The converse, having a representation in which all JNDs are the same size plus Weber's Law does not imply Fechner's Law, as was shown in footnote 9. A general characterization of JND representations using functional equations is described in Luce and Edwards (1958).

5

Measurement Essentials in a Nutshell

Measurement is concerned with how numbers enter into science. For the next few chapters, we only need two essential concepts of measurement theory. These are *scale types* and correlative *meaningfulness*. We discuss general measurement issues more fully later, in Chapters 10 and 11.

In science, we study various empirical operations and relations between objects. Sometimes it is useful to map objects in the world onto numbers, such that mathematical operations and relations between the numbers mirror the empirical operations and relations. This is just what measurement, in the most general sense, is. But numbers have lots of structure, some are prime, some are cube roots of others, and so on... Some of the structure will be superfluous to the task of mirroring an empirical structure. In other words, alternative mappings of objects to numbers may do the job just as well. Three children go to a playground, sit on a seesaw, and lift their feet. Nancy always goes up. Gordo always goes down. Rebecca goes down against Nancy but up against Gordo. This little experiment gives us an empirical ordering: ⟨Gordo, Rebecca, Nancy⟩. We can represent this order by mapping into numbers and using the numerical order to represent the empirical order. This can done equally well in many ways, with the numbers being assigned to Gordo, Rebecca, Nancy being respectively ⟨4, 3, 2⟩, or ⟨34, 21, 13⟩, or ⟨11, 7, 5⟩, or ⟨100, 99, 1⟩.

An important concept we use through this book is "weak order." It describes attributes whose elements can be ordered on a line, but allowing for multiple elements to occupy the same position. We say a precedes b if a comes before b on the line, in symbols, $a \prec b$; a is equivalent to b if they occupy the same position on the line, in symbols, $a \sim b$; and a succeeds b if a comes after b on the line, in symbols, $a \succ b$. Then, for every two elements a and b of the attribute, either a precedes b or a is equivalent to b or a succeeds b. An example of a weak order is the attribute of weight. It can be thought of as being on a line. Let M stand for Mary and J for John. Then it is a prototypical property of weight that either Mary weighs less than John, or Mary and John have the same weight, or Mary weighs more than John; in symbols,

The Pursuit of Happiness: Philosophical and Psychological Foundations of Utility. Louis Narens and Brian Skyrms, Oxford University Press (2020). © Louis Narens and Brian Skyrms.
DOI: 10.1093/oso/9780198856450.001.0001

$$M \prec J \text{ or } M \sim J \text{ or } M \succ J.$$

We use the notation $M \precsim J$ to say "Mary's weight is less than or is the same as John's." If all that matters is the order, transforming one scale that does the job to any that preserves the order (a monotonic transformation) gives an assignment that does the job equally as well.

We define *scale types* by the kind of transformations on the numbers that do the job as representing the empirical structure just as well. Here the scale type was *ordinal*.

A range of different scales of measurement, reflecting more or less empirical content, are possible. For instance, one can think of temperature scales before and after the establishment of an absolute zero. Before, it was an *interval scale*—that is, its scale consisted of all transformations of the form $x \rightarrow rx+s$, with r positive and s real, of any of its *representations*, for example, the Centigrade representation. After, it became a *ratio scale*—that is, its scale family consisted of all transformations of the form $x \rightarrow rx$, r positive, of any one of its representations, for example, the Kelvin representation. More empirical structure corresponds to smaller classes of transformations preserving it. The smallest class consists of the identity transformation, and its scale type is said to be *absolute*. The largest ordered class consists of all strictly increasing transformations is called an *ordinal scale*.

To summarize, the most important scales to appear in science consist of scales types with the following transformations:

- *ordinal scales*: $x \rightarrow f(x)$, f a strictly increasing function,
- *interval scales*: $x \rightarrow rx + s$, r positive, s real,
- *ratio scales*:[1] $x \rightarrow rx$, r positive,
- *absolute scales*: $x \rightarrow x$.

Meaningful numerical properties, or statistics, or judgments are those that remain invariant over the appropriate class of scale transformations. It would be meaningless to compare the average weights of boys and girls in the playground if all we had was an ordinal scale. It is meaningful to say that the temperature today is 10 percent higher today than yesterday if we are measuring temperature on a ratio scale (Kelvin), but it is meaningless if we

---

[1] There are various kinds of ratio scales depending on whether there are 0 or negative elements. Some ratio scales are onto the positive real numbers, others onto all reals, and others onto the non-negative reals.

are just dealing with an interval scale, because then Fahrenheit and Celsius are equally good.

It is evidently of some importance that in discussing Utilitarian issues one needs to be clear about the sort of scale on which utilities are supposed to be measured. Some philosophers are not so careful about this. For instance, popular "counterexamples" to Utilitarianism such as Robert Nozick's "Utility Monster" and Derek Parfit's "Repugnant Conclusion" implicitly make strong assumptions about utility scales. We will discuss these later.

6

Skeptics

Recall the anonymous critic of Jevons, quoted by Edgeworth:

> We can tell that one pleasure is greater than another; but that does not help us. To apply the mathematical methods, pleasure must be in some way capable of numerical expression; we must be able to say, for example, that the pleasure of eating a beefsteak is to the pleasure of drinking a glass of beer as five to four.

The critic is demanding that utility be measured on a ratio scale. It must be meaningful to say that one pleasure is to another in the ratio five to four. This is what was meant by "cardinal utility" in the nineteenth century.

6.1 Skeptics

Although some Utilitarians thought that measurement on a ratio scale could be achieved by techniques of psychophysics, there were skeptics who did not have so much faith in psychological science. The skeptics, including the anonymous critic of Jevons, thought that ordering of pleasures and pains was a far as utility measurement could go. Utility could, at best, be measured on an ordinal scale. Eventually it became clear that much of extant economic theory required no more than an ordinal theory, and many economists eschewed old-fashioned Utilitarianism as unscientific. The unscientific elements to be discarded apparently included the rationale for social reform that had animated early Utilitarianism. Their passing was regarded with various degrees of wistfulness and attempted rationalization. This was the ordinal revolution in economics. The possibility of measurement between ordinal and ratio scales was really not in the conceptual space of theoreticians at the time.

This is not to say that participants in the ordinal revolution were all the same. The evolution of views of utility from nineteenth-century Cardinalism to Ordinalism, and the varieties of Ordinalism that resulted is well-illustrated

The Pursuit of Happiness: Philosophical and Psychological Foundations of Utility. Louis Narens and Brian Skyrms, Oxford University Press (2020). © Louis Narens and Brian Skyrms.
DOI: 10.1093/oso/9780198856450.001.0001

by the Austrian school of economics, centered at the University of Vienna. The Austrian school of economics shared both time and place with the Logical Empiricist school of philosophy—the "Vienna Circle."[1] The philosophers wanted to make philosophy scientific; the economists wanted to make economics scientific.

Scientific philosophy at the University of Vienna had actually been inaugurated by two physicists. In 1895, Ernst Mach was appointed Professor in the History and Philosophy of the Inductive Sciences. When Mach retired due to health issues in 1902, Ludwig Boltzmann lectured in physics and philosophy until his death in 1906. Interest in scientific philosophy continued at the university, and what is known as the Vienna Circle of philosophy coalesced around Moritz Schlick, who joined the university in 1922. The circle included physicists, mathematicians, philosophers, and social scientists. Among the latter was Oskar Morgenstern, who later—at Princeton—inaugurated modern utility theory in collaboration with John von Neumann.

Morgenstern was an economist, and economists had their own circle, which met regularly at the university. The Austrian school of economics was founded in the 1870's by Carl Menger. It continued with the University of Vienna as its center until its members, like the philosophers of the Vienna circle, were scattered with the rise of the Nazis.[2]

Menger did not discuss measurability of utility, but his work tacitly assumed measurement on a classical cardinal scale, that is to say on a ratio scale, just like length. His student, Böhm-Bawerk, however, explicitly argued for measurability of utility, against the skeptical stance taken by a contemporary German economist. The argument is that one must be able to measure utilities on a ratio scale in order to choose. A boy faced with the choice of eating an apple or six plums must ask whether the pleasure of eating an apple is more or less than six times the pleasure of eating a plum.[3] This argument was decisively answered by his student, Ludwig von Mises, who held that utility could not be measured, but could only be ordered. To decide, the boy would not need to perform arithmetic on the utility of a plum, which in any case, need not be constant. He need only order the utilities of (A) eating six plums and (B) eating one apple. Ordering of alternatives is all that is needed for choice.[4]

---

[1] On the history of the Vienna circle, we highly recommend Karl Sigmund's (2017) *Exact Thinking in Demented Times*.

[2] On the measurability of utility in the Austrian school, see Moscati 2015. Now superseded by Moscati's splendid book *Measuring Utility* (2018).

[3] See Moscati (2018: 10).

[4] Von Mises (1912).

6.2 Indifference Curves

In fact, it slowly became clear that ordering was all that was needed for a lot of existing economic theory. Equilibrium is a notion that only needs ordering; no agent is better off by deviating.[5] Indifference is a notion that only depends on ordering. The indifference curve analysis that Edgeworth (1888 [1881]) had developed in his *Mathematical Psychics* on the basis of Bentham's cardinal utility was redone using only ordinal utility by a series of economists.

An indifference curve for Edgeworth was a way of visualizing tradeoffs between goods for an individual. Points on the same curve represent bundles of goods which, for the agent, have the same utility—see Figure 6.1.

The pivotal figure in the ordinal revolution was an Italian engineer, turned economist in his 40s, Vilfredo Pareto. Pareto did not take utility of any kind as a basic concept to explain behavior. Rather he built up his theory on "the naked fact of choice."[6] Behavior was basic. Ordinal utility could be built up from dispositions to choose. We see a radical shift, philosophically as well as technically, from the psychological hedonism of the English Utilitarians. Pareto, like the Vienna Circle, was interested in bringing scientific rigor to his discipline. Basing economics on introspective psychology was to be avoided.

The ordinal revolution was later solidified by two economists in England, Hicks and Allen. Here is their assessment of Pareto's pivotal work:

> Of all Pareto's contributions there is probably none that exceeds in importance his demonstration of the immeasurability of utility. To most earlier writers, to Marshall, to Walras, to Edgeworth, utility had been a quantity theoretically measurable; that is to say, a quantity which would be measurable if we had enough facts. Pareto definitely abandoned this, and replaced the concept of utility by the concept of a scale of preferences.[7]

They emphasize that Pareto did more than simply postulate an ordinal scale, he showed what could be done with it:

> It is not always observed that this change in concepts was not merely a change of view, a pure matter of methodology; it rested on a positive

[5] Pointed out by Irving Fisher in (1982) "Mathematical Investigations into the Theory of Price".

[6] Letter to Pantaleoni (1899), quoted in Pareto (2010).

[7] Hicks and Allen (1934: 52).

Example of choice of goods which give consumers the same utility

Apples	Bananas
22	17
14	20
10	26
9	41
7	80

Table plotted as indifference curve

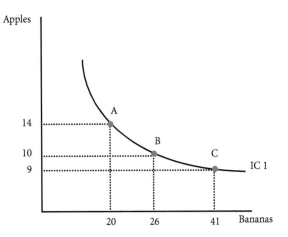

Figure 6.1 Indifference curve A. Assuming that more is better, we get nested indifference curves. Diminishing marginal utility for each of the goods gives the indifference curves a convex shape.

demonstration that the facts of observable conduct make a scale of preferences capable of theoretical construction . . . but they do not enable us to proceed from the scale of preference to a particular utility function.

6.3 Two Kinds of Ordinalism

By the end of the First World War, most economists had become Ordinalists. But ordinalism could mean different things. Some of the Vienna school, including Oscar Morgenstern, held that it was meaningful not only to order utilities, but also differences in utilities.[8] Taking the differences very small and a little idealization kept ordering of marginal utilities as

---

[8] Pareto thought the same.

Indifference curve map

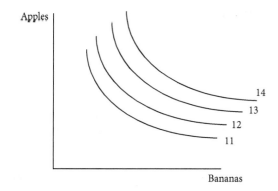

Figure 6.2 Indifference curve B. We can also show different indifference curves. All choices on 12 give the same utility. But, it will be a higher net utility than indifference curve 11; 14 gives the highest net utility. Basically, 14 would require higher income than 11.

Budget line

A budget line shows the combination of goods that can be afforded with your current income.

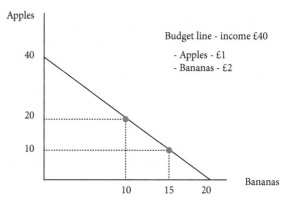

Figure 6.3 Budget line. A budget line shows the combination of goods that can be afforded with your current income. If an apple costs £1 and a banana £2, the above budget line shows all the combinations of the goods which can be bought with £40. For example: (i) 20 apples at £1 and 10 bananas at £2 versus (ii) 10 apples at £1 and 15 bananas at £2.

Optimal choice of goods for consumer

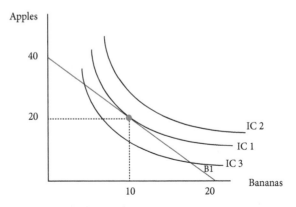

Figure 6.4 Optimal choice of goods for consumer. Given a budget line of B1, the consumer will maximize utility where the highest indifference curve is tangential to the budget line (20 apples, 10 bananas). Given current income, IC2 is unobtainable. IC3 is obtainable but gives less utility than the higher IC1.

meaningful. They could be used to define equilibria. The hypothesis of decreasing marginal utility could be used. This was, they thought, still just ordering—not measuring—utility.

The magnitude of the step was not realized because they did not have the benefit of the perspective of modern measurement theory. If only total utilities can be ordered, then orderings on differences of utility are not meaningful. If situation A is preferred to B, B to C, C to D, then the ordering is preserved by giving them utilities respectively 4, 3, 2, 0, but the ordering is equally well-preserved by assigning utilities 4, 2, 1, 0. If we ask how the difference $u(A) - u(B)$ compares with the difference $u(C) - u(D)$, the two assignments give different answers. The meaningfulness of ordering of utility differences requires measuring utility on a stronger scale. How much stronger?

6.3.1 Enter the Interval Scale: Franz Alt

Morgenstern felt that he did not know enough mathematics, and engaged a young mathematician, Franz Alt, to tutor him.[9] Through Morgenstern, Alt

---

[9] See Moscati (2018).

became interested in the measurement of utility, and in particular, in what is required for the meaningful ordering of utility differences and transitions. Alt published his conclusions in a short article in Morgenstern's journal.[10] This paper has a remarkably modern flavor. It begins with a precise statement of what he meant by measurement, which is worth reproducing here:

> When we say the utility of a commodity is "measurable" or "numerically representable" we mean that we can assign a real number to each commodity and to each set of commodities, which is called the utility of the commodity, respectively the set of commodities, in such a way that this assignment is unique, except for the choice of origin and unit of measurement.
>
> (pp. 425–6)

Alt defines measurement not in the ratio scale sense current in the nineteenth-century economics of Bentham and Edgeworth, but rather in the sense of an interval scale. This is the type of scale that Von Neumann and Morgenstern later developed using chance to measure utility. (We discuss the Von Neumann-Morgenstern theory in Section 7.1.) Alt went on to prove that if both total utility and utility differences could be ordered, if the orderings were consistent with one another, and a few other conditions hold, then utility is measurable on an interval scale.[11] The importance of Alt's theory is that he showed that assumptions that were commonly used in practice by some Ordinalists led to interval-scaled utility, and this made Morgenstern aware that interval-scaled utility had a serious mathematical foundation.

---

[10] Alt (1971 [1936]: 425–31).

[11] Alt wanted his assumptions to be simple and equivalent to the existence of interval-scale utility for commodities. Besides standard assumptions about the divisibility of commodities and topological convergence, he made behavioral assumptions about their exchangeability and a theoretical assumption about the existence of an equally spaced sequence of commodities in terms of their utilities. The exchangeability allowed a weak ordering to be constructed, that is, commodity b is preferred to commodity a if and only if the person is willing to exchange a to get b. It is the sequence of equally space commodities that drives the system to interval scalability. This principle was not derived from behavioral axioms. Alt only noted that it was "frequently accepted and even applied by opponents of measurability of utility." This is the major weakness of his theory. For the situation considered by Alt, behavioral axioms for the equal spacing of commodities were presented about thirty years later by Luce and Tukey (1964), in their seminal article on additive conjoint measurement (e.g., see Section 10.4 of this book) and were later applied later for the measurement of the ordering of differences (e.g., see Krantz et al. 1971: ch. 4).

Economists now call it cardinal utility. Interval-scaled utility that was ordinal utility in Vienna in 1936 became cardinal utility in Princeton in 1947.[12]

6.4 Orthodox Ordinalists

But before the Von Neumann-Morgenstern collaboration, Ordinalists, by and large, abandoned ordering of utility differences. Hicks and Allen solidified the reduction of standard economic theory to purely ordinal utility measurement without any use of utility differences. Indifference need not be based on utility measurement; it is a purely ordinal notion. Preference is the ordinal notion that gives us higher and lower indifference curves. Indifference curves cannot cross because that would violate the transitivity of indifference.[13] Convexity of indifference curves cannot be based on diminishing marginal utility of each of the goods, because this makes no sense on the purely ordinal view of utility. But it can be taken directly as a fact about the preferences over bundles of goods. Indifference curves for two agents can likewise be used to analyze barter. All that is required is a preference ordering over bundles of goods for each of the agents.

6.5 Pareto Dominance

If diminishing marginal utility no longer makes sense, what is left of Utilitarian ethics? Bentham based egalitarian social policies on the greatest happiness principle together with diminishing marginal utility of money and of the goods that money can buy. On the purely ordinal view of utility, only a shadow of the greatest happiness principle remains meaningful. That is Pareto optimality: Social state A Pareto dominates social state B, if at least one member of society prefers A to B, and other members of society either also prefer A to B or are indifferent between the two.

A state is Pareto optimal if no other state Pareto dominates it. Pareto optimality is meaningful, since it only depends on individuals' preference

---

[12] Alternate versions interval cardinality not based on chance were later develop in the 1960s by measurement theorists. They are discussed in Krantz et al. (1971: ch. 4). They are simpler and more behavioral than Alt's.

[13] Transitivity of indifference and other ordering properties are questionable empirical assumptions. Empirical intransitivity of indifference was later addressed by Duncan Luce (1956) in his theory of semiorders, which is discussed in Chapter 11.

orderings, but it provides rather weak guidance. If all we were to care about is how many goats we own, then the state where you own all the goats would Pareto optimal, as would be the state where I own them all. So would be the state where we each own half, or when you own $\frac{2}{3}$ of them and I own $\frac{1}{3}$. If it is good to honor individuals' preferences, and A Pareto dominates B, then A is a better social state then B. But following one path of Pareto improvements or another may lead a society to quite different places.

This can be illustrated using indifference curves in an ingenious setup invented by Edgeworth, and utilized by Pareto and by subsequent generations of economists: *the Edgeworth box*. Consider two individuals engaged in barter between two goods. There are fixed quantities of the two goods available, with proportions of the total. The proportions of the two goods held by Mary are graphed on the X and Y axes, respectively. Mary has indifference curves as before. What is not held by Mary is held by Jane, so flipping the origin from southwest to northeast gives the proportions held by Jane. Jane has indifference curves as well. For Mary moving to new indifference curves to the northeast is better; for Jane moving to indifference curves to the southwest is preferred.

Holdings of Mary and Jane can thus be specified by a single point in the box. Suppose that the initial holdings are specified by a point, and the respective indifference curves through that point, are as shown in Figure 6.5.

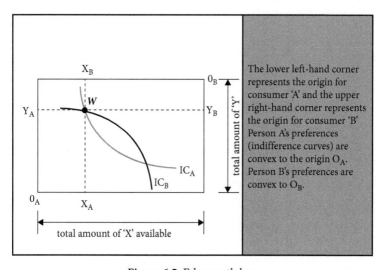

Figure 6.5 Edgeworth box.

Then any point inside the lens-shaped area enclosed by the curves Pareto dominates the initial point. Any such point makes both individuals better off, according to their preferences. It is to their mutual advantage to trade.

They may trade and still be in a similar situation, in which case they will trade again. The only equilibrium is at a point where Mary's indifference curve just kisses that of Jane. Such a point is Pareto optimal, and neither has any incentive to trade. But in the situation depicted, there is a whole line of such Pareto optimal equilibria through the lens-shaped area, and which point barter will lead to is indeterminate. This is illustrated in Figure 6.6 where a curve of points where indifference curves kiss is traced out.

This much reasoning about general welfare can be done with purely ordinal utility using Pareto dominance. The extent to which this line of thought generalizes is the subject of modern welfare economics. Equilibrium in trade leading to a Pareto Optimal outcome is generalized to idealized exchange economies. Given, we must emphasize, very considerable idealization, trade leads to a Pareto optimal equilibrium and any Pareto optimal equilibrium can be reached by trade starting from some initial endowment. Thus Pareto optimality does little to solve the problems of social reform that motivated the classical Utilitarians. Something more is required for Utilitarian ethics to have much bite. Lionel Robbins (1938), a convinced skeptic about both cardinal utility and interpersonal comparability, writes:

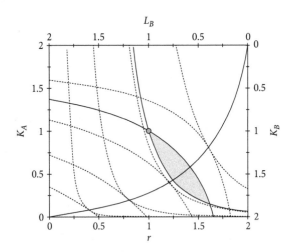

Figure 6.6 Curve of mutual advantage.

My own attitude to problems of political action has always been one of what I might call provisional utilitarianism.... I have always felt that, as a first approximation in handling questions relating to the lives and actions of large masses of people, the approach which counts each man as one and, on that assumption, asks which way lies the greatest happiness, is less likely to lead one astray than any of the absolute systems....

Would it not be better, I asked myself, quite frankly to acknowledge that the postulate for equal satisfaction *came from the outside*, and that it rested upon ethical principle rather than scientific demonstration, that it was not judgment of fact in the scientific sense, but rather a judgment of value— perhaps even, in the last analysis, an act of will?

1938: pp 635-7

Here we have a pragmatic ethical stance to a modified Utilitarianism, that is a move away from Edgeworth and perhaps closer to Bentham. Equality between individuals is a postulate, but it is an ethical postulate rather than an empirical one. But exactly what units are postulated equal: JND or ... ? We are back to the measurement question.

Appendix 6.1. Revealed Preference

The Pareto program was pushed even further by the American economist Paul Samuelson. Samuelson begins his 1938 paper by calling into question the whole Utilitarian program of basing utility measurement on psychology:

The discrediting of utility as a psychological concept robbed it of its only possible virtue as an explanation of human behavior ....

(p. 61)

He thought that postulation of a utility ordering was too far removed from observable behavior:

Consistently applied, however, the modern criticism turns back on itself and cuts deeply. For just as we do not claim to know by introspection the behavior of utility, many will argue we cannot know the behavior of ratios of marginal utilities, or of indifference directions.

(p. 61)

The claim of not knowing utility preference orderings by introspection, and arguing that they should instead be derived from observable behavior is the program of "revealed preference" Samuelson inaugurated. It was furthered by a whole string of researchers who followed him.

Here is the leading idea. An individual is presented with a set of alternatives and chooses some subset. If things work out, this is thought of as an optimal subset, with members being preferred to non-members, and indifference between members. An individual can make this choice for any set with which she is presented. Given certain consistency conditions, these choices generate an ordinal utility scale, such that individuals choose what they prefer. (For more detail, see Appendix 6.2 for revealed preference.) The consistency conditions themselves are empirical hypotheses. It is logically possible for choice behavior to violate them, in which case ordinal utilities would not exist. The theory should be applied where they are not violated. This is close to Pareto's goal of building the theory on the "naked fact of choice."

However, the theory requires many more choices than an individual in real life actually gets to make. It is built on dispositions to choose rather than actual choices. Is there a certain residue of psychology hidden behind Samuelson's appeal to actual choice behavior? One could answer by saying that the actual choices that an individual does make, given consistency, can be embedded in an ordinal utility function. The ordering represents the choices. But the representing preference ordering is not uniquely determined. There is a class of preference orderings corresponding to actual behavior. Here the data are just the naked fact of choices made. Of course, it is still possible to make inductive inferences and predict the outcomes of choice situations not already encountered.

From this point of view, economics has been purged of psychology. What of ethics? From a revealed preference point of view, it is hard to see how even Pareto dominance retains any bite. There is no underlying reality to the preferences, they are just a bit of mathematics behind choice behavior. The point has been made forcefully by Samuelson (1938):

> In closing, I should like to state my personal opinion that nothing said here in the field of consumers' behavior affects in any way, or touches upon, at any point the problem of welfare economics, except in the sense of revealing the confusion in the traditional theory of these distinct subjects.

> (p. 71)

Appendix 6.2. Revealed Preference Worked Out

Here is a simple sample.

We have a finite global set of alternatives. For some non-empty subsets, S_i, of the global set, the decision maker has a choice function f, which maps S_i onto a chosen subset $f(S_i)$. If an alternative, x, is in $f(S_i)$, we say that x is *chosen* from S_i. The first question that arises in whether the choices given by the choice function can represented as coming from a preference ordering. If so it is said to be *rationalizable*. Not every choice function is rationalizable. For instance if a is chosen from $\{a, b\}$, b is chosen from $\{b, c\}$, and c is chosen from $\{a, c\}$ the choice function in question is not rationalizable.

A nice way to present conditions under which a choice function is rationalizable is due to the economist Amartya Sen (1971), who breaks an earlier answer into pieces:

- α: If x is chosen from a set B, A is a subset of B and x is in A, then x is chosen from A.

The thought is that if x is as good as anything in B it must be as good as anything in A since everything in A is a subset of B.

- β: If x and y are both chosen from A, and A is a subset of B, and x is chosen from B, then y is also chosen from B.

The thought is the if x and y are tied from being the best in A, and x is still best in the larger set B, then y must still be tied with x for best in B. Should the choice function always pick a singleton, β is vacuously satisfied.

If a choice function satisfies α and β, then it is rationalizable.

Let $w \precsim z$ stand for "z is weakly preferred to w." Then $\precsim$ is defined as follows:

- $x \precsim x$, and
- if x is chosen from the set $\{x, y\}$, then $y \precsim x$.

The key property that needs to be demonstrated is that $\precsim$ is transitive. Suppose not. Then there are x, y, and z such that x is chosen from $\{x, y\}$, y is chosen from $\{y, z\}$, but x is not chosen from $\{x, z\}$. We are then led to ask what is chosen from $\{x, y, z\}$. The reader can check that any answer violates either α or β.

If a choice function is rationalizable, one may ask whether the preference ordering that rationalizes it is uniquely determined. So far we have left open the question: For which subsets of the global set is the choice function defined? If it is defined for all subsets, then the ordering over the global set that rationalizes the choice function is uniquely determined.

Conversely, you can verify that a complete preference ordering over the global set of alternatives induces a choice function on all subsets that satisfies Sen's α and β.

To the extent that α and β qualify as rationality principles, they justify the term "rationalizable" as applied to choice functions. To the extent that they hold empirically in some domain, they support the use of ordinal utilities in modeling that domain.

7

Using Chance to Measure Utility

7.1 Von Neumann-Morgenstern

"Posterity may regard this book as one of the great intellectual achievements of the first half of the twentieth century." That is how the mathematician Arthur Copeland began his review of Von Neumann and Morgenstern's 1944 *Theory of Games and Economic Behavior.* Copeland starts by discussing the theory of utility measurement created in that book:

> The authors observe that the give-and-take of business has many of the aspects of a game and they make an extensive study of the strategy of games with this similarity in mind (hence the title of this book). In the game of life, the stakes are not necessarily monetary; they may be merely utilities. In discussing utilities, the authors find it advisable to replace the questionable marginal utility theory by a new theory which is more suitable to their analysis. They note that in the game of life as well as in social games the players are frequently called upon to choose between alternatives to which probabilities rather than certainties are attached.

Morgenstern was an economist with strong philosophical interests. In 1928, he published a book on economic forecasting that made a distinction between live and dead variables. Dead variables may be uncertain, but are fixed—like the weather next year. Live variables come from the actions of other economic agents that are also attempting to optimize. When a number of live variables interact, we are in the realm of what later became called the theory of games. Games of strategy are prime examples. Morgenstern thought that optimization problems among live variables could be in principle insoluble. What is optimal for A depends on what B does, and what is optimal for B depends on what A does. In cases of diametrically opposed interests, there may be no solution that is optimal for both. Morgenstern used as an illustration Sherlock Holmes and Dr Moriarty trying to outguess each other. He concluded that in such cases, prediction of the behavior of optimizing agents is impossible. This seemingly paradoxical result was repeated

The Pursuit of Happiness: Philosophical and Psychological Foundations of Utility. Louis Narens and Brian Skyrms,
Oxford University Press (2020). © Louis Narens and Brian Skyrms.
DOI: 10.1093/oso/9780198856450.001.0001

in a paper of 1935, and discussed by philosophers in Moritz Schlick's Vienna Circle seminar, and economists in Karl Menger's seminar at the University of Vienna. In the latter meeting, a young mathematician told Morgenstern that John von Neumann had discussed the same issue in a paper of 1928, the same year as Morgenstern's book.

This was Von Neumann's first paper on the theory of games, in which he proved his famous minimax theorem. This paper contained a solution to Morgenstern's paradox. In games of diametrically opposed interests, zero-sum games, a combination of strategies where all players optimize against the others does indeed exist, provided that players can use randomized strategies rather than the deterministic strategies that were considered by Morgenstern. There is therefore a reason intrinsic to the theory, to "choose between alternatives to which probabilities rather than certainties are attached."

But despite this commonality of interest, the two did not meet in Europe. Von Neumann had turned his attention to other things in mathematics, Morgenstern to other things in economics. Hitler intervened. As a result of the annexation of Austria by Nazi Germany, Von Neumann and Morgenstern both ended up at Princeton—Morgenstern in the economics department of the university, Von Neumann at the Institute for Advanced Study. Then met, became good friends, and decided to write a joint paper on the theory of games. As they talked and worked together, the paper grew into a very long paper, then a monograph, and eventually a book.

Optimization presupposes some quantity to optimize. Von Neumann and Morgenstern needed numbers for their payoffs. Morgenstern recalls discussing the question while on vacation with Von Neumann:

> Among the things that came up very early was that we were in need of a number for the pay-off matrices. We had the choice of merely putting in a number, calling it money, and making money equal for both participants and unrestrictedly transferable. I was not very happy about this, knowing the importance of the utility concept, and I insisted that we do more. At first, we were intending merely to postulate a numerical utility, but then I said that, as I knew my fellow economists, they would find this impossible to accept and old-fashioned.
>
> (Morgenstern 1976: 805)

As we have seen in Chapter 5, the measurement of utility was indeed a sensitive question for economists, and especially economists of the Austrian school. The dominant view was that utilities were only ordinally measurable. One could say one utility was greater than another, but not by how much. Morgenstern himself was still regarded as in the ordinal camp.[1] The discussion of the nature of utility in economics had been on an informal, philosophical plane. With Von Neumann that was not good enough. One needed an axiomatic treatment of the utility concept to be used in game theory. Morgenstern recounts:

> ... the construction of axioms for our expected utility came quite naturally. I recall vividly how Johnny rose from our table when we had set down the axioms and called out in astonishment: "Ja hat denn das niemand gesehen?" ("But didn't anyone see that?").[2]

The natural idea was to use to use probability to measure utility. The bridge between the two was the expectation principle: the value of a gamble is the probability weighted average of payoffs. This had been used since the birth of probability theory with the analysis of gambles by Cardano, Galileo, Pascal, and Fermat. It was applied to gambles with non-monetary outcomes by Cramer and Bernoulli in their analysis of the St Petersburg game. This was well-known to Morgenstern through Karl Menger's[3] 1934 paper on the subject.[4] But we don't know the values of the gambles, so how can we use them to measure the chances. The answer that Von Neumann and Morgenstern came up with is a mix of cardinal and ordinal ideas.

The agent in question is assumed at the onset to have only ordinal utilities, but they are utilities over gambles over the outcomes. That is, the agent has a complete preference ordering over these gambles. If the preference ordering meets some additional conditions, numerical utilities for the chances are deduced. The starting ordering of gambles is then recovered as the numerical order of their expected utilities.

Chance and the expectation principle are used to measure utility. What kind of measurement is it? It is not cardinal measurement in the sense supposed by the early Cardinalists of the Austrian school; it is not like the measurement of length. Rather the utilities gotten by Von Neumann and Morgensterm are unique only up to an arbitrary choice of zero and unit,

---

[1] See Moscati (2015) for more detail.
[2] Morgenstern (1976: 809).
[3] Menger (1934). Karl Menger was the son of Carl Menger.
[4] See Morgenstern (1976).

like the choice of a temperature scale before the discovery of absolute zero. Utilities are measured on an interval scale.

The numbers cannot be more constrained because the expectation principle is being used to measure utilities. Multiply all utilities of all outcomes by a positive constant and then add a constant, and you get the same ordering of gambles by expected utility. So the scale of all expected utility representations is an interval scale.

We pause in this exposition to emphasize two points. The first is, as we have said, that the expectation principle is presupposed in the Von Neumann-Morgenstern representation. Preferences over gambles are recovered as numerical ordering of expected utilities. Any order-preserving transformation of expected utilities of gambles would also preserve preferences. So we could have all sorts of other representations of the preferences over gambles. We may, however, have other reasons to hold fast to the expectation principle—as early probabilists noted. On a long series of independent trials, maximizing expectation on individual trials predicts maximum total payoff. In this sense, maximizing expectation can be seen as a good rule. The second is that the theorem does not preclude the possibility of extending the measurement of utility on a scale having fewer representations, for example, a ratio scale, by some supplemental means that goes beyond preferences. But it calls into question the usefulness of any such extension. For if choice is by maximizing expected utility, what behavioral consequences could the stronger measurement have? We will give an answer to this question in our chapter on convention. In cases of social interaction, what maximizes your utility may depend on what I do, and what maximizes my utility may depend on what you do. In this case, stronger measurement of utility by a social convention might support both mutual inference and maximization.

We now need to prove that there *exists* a utility assignment that does the trick in the first place. We illustrate with a simplified version of the proof for the case where there are only a finite number of possible outcomes. The agent under consideration has preferences of all possible gambles, that is to say over all possible probability assignments over possible outcomes. The preferences of an ideal agent are assumed to satisfy:

(1) *Ordering:* For any two gambles, p and p', either p is preferred to p', or p' is preferred to p or the agent is indifferent between p and p'.

(2) *Continuity:* If p is preferred to p' and p' is preferred to p'', then there is a probability a such that the agent is indifferent between the gambles:

$$ap + (1 - a)p'' \text{ and } p'.$$

(3) *Independence:* p is preferred to p' if and only if:

$$ap + (1 - a)p'' \text{ is preferred to } ap' + (1 - a)p''$$

for all a and all p''.

The ordering axiom says that the ideal agent has thought things through. She is not simply befuddled, not knowing what to prefer or what to take as of equal value. Continuity assumes that with all possible gambles in play, we can narrow down a value gap to exactly match something of intermediate value. Independence rests on the thought if we get p'' in each case, it cancels out and preference must go by the preference of p over p'.

Given a preference ordering that satisfied these axioms, we construct a utility. Assume we are not indifferent between all outcomes. Since we have a finite number of outcomes, there must be one (or more) maximally preferred ones, the Best. And there must be one or more minimally preferred one (or ones), the Worst. We will say that Best have utility 1 and Worst have utility zero. Gambles between Best and Worst which give probability p to Best and $1 - p$ to Worst are, in accordance with the expectation principle, given utility p.

How do we know that this is legitimate, that it is faithful to your preferences? For instance, how do we know that you really prefer Best to a non-trivial gamble between Best and Worst: $p \cdot \text{Best} + (1 - p) \cdot \text{Worst}$. Observe that Best for sure is equivalent to $p \cdot (\text{Best}) + (1 - p) \cdot \text{Best}$. Now, by independence:

$$p \cdot \text{Best} + (1 - p) \cdot \text{Best}$$

is preferred to

$$p \cdot \text{Best} + (1 - p) \cdot \text{Worst},$$

because the first term cancels out and Best is preferred to Worst. More reasoning of this kind shows that our utility scale for these special gambles between Best and Worst faithfully reproduce the preferences over them with which we started.

There may be many outcomes other than Best and Worst, and gambles between all outcomes. The utility of any such gamble is assigned matching it to one on the scale that we have just established, such that it is a matter of indifference between this other gamble and the one already on our scale. That there always is one is assured by continuity.

This also has to be proved to be faithful to the original preferences, with higher utility numbers corresponding to preferred gambles. This is accomplished by repeated application of ordering, continuity, and independence.

After *Theory of Games and Economic Behavior* was published, this quickly became the standard account of utility theory in economics. Von Neumann was the foremost mathematician of the time; Morgenstern was an Austrian economist identified with Ordinalism. The distinguished economist, Paul Samuelson, initially objected to independence, but then became convinced in correspondence with Savage that it was indeed a rationality axiom.[5] Utility, as measured on an interval scale, was now widely regarded as legitimate. Economists now call this cardinal utility. But it is not the cardinal utility of early Austrian economists, which required a ratio scale. Rather, it corresponded to one version of Ordinalism, indeed that of Morgenstern.[6] The revolution was not from ordinal to cardinal, but rather a conceptual revolution that founded interval-scale utility on a rigorous mathematical basis.

Observe that the focus has now shifted from psychology to rationality. The psychological plausibility of each of the three axioms listed above is questionable. Individuals may be at a loss when called upon to order all gambles among outcomes. Any sort of granularity of value, or JND, seems to argue against continuity. An example of Maurice Allais shows that many people violate independence. As a rationality principle independence has also generated discussion, centered on examples of Maurice Allais and Daniel Ellsberg. Alternative utility theories that violate independence have been constructed. Von Neumann-Morgenstern, however, remains the standard theory in economics. Utility theory has now moved quite a distance from the concerns of Bentham. It no longer makes any attempt to measure the psychological sensation of pleasure.

In a note, Von Neumann and Morgenstern say that it would be possible to develop a theory of subjective probability and utility. In his 1976 memoir,

---

[5] See Moscati (2018), who quotes from letters between the two.
[6] See the discussions of Morgenstern and Alt in Chapter 5.

Morgenstern remarks that "this was done later by others."[7] In fact, it was done earlier in a paper read to the Moral Sciences Club at Cambridge in 1926. This is Frank Plumpton Ramsey's "Truth and Probability."[8]

7.2 Ramsey

Ramsey invented a subjective surrogate for the objective chances that Von Neumann and Morgenstern used to scale utilities. The clever key idea is that of an ethically neutral proposition. A proposition is ethically neutral for an agent if, for every possible consequence, the agent is indifferent to having the consequence if the proposition is true, and having the consequence if the proposition is false. In a gamble, a result of a coin flip or a throw of the dice is usually treated as ethically neutral. The gambler doesn't care about heads or tails itself; he cares about what he wins or loses.

Suppose I do prefer outcome A to outcome B, and suppose that I have an ethically neutral proposition, H, such that I am indifferent between A if H, B if not, and B if H, A if not. Then subjectively I am treating H as an ethically neutral proposition with probability one-half. I have a subjective surrogate for a fair coin flip. (A flip of a coin that the agent takes to be fair is a plausible candidate.) Given a stock of such ethically neutral propositions, Ramsey is able to measure utility much as Von Neumann and Morgenstern did later.

"Ja hat denn das niemand gesehen?" ("But didn't anyone see that?"). Ramsey did, but Ramsey's great insight passed almost unnoticed until his work was rediscovered by Savage. After Savage had completed his simultaneous derivation of subjective probability and utility,[9] he decided to see what philosophers had to say on the subject. He found Ramsey, the importance of whom philosophers by and large had missed, and made his contributions known:

> Ramsey improves on Bernoulli in that he defines utility operationally in terms of the behavior of a person constrained by certain postulates. Ramsey's essays, though now much appreciated, seem to have had relatively little influence.
>
> (p. 96)

---

[7] Morgenstern (1976: 810).

[8] Ramsey (1926).

[9] See Savage (1954).

Let us sketch a little more about Ramsey that will connect with what follows. You might imagine that Ramsey would try to get a subjective surrogate for a roulette wheel or wheel of fortune from ethically neutral propositions. There would be N possible outcomes ordered by strict preference—each strictly preferred to those below it. The subject would be indifferent between the gamble that gives outcome 1 if ethically neutral proposition 1, 2 if ethically neutral proposition 2, etc., and all gambles gotten from these by permutation of outcomes. Then all the ethically neutral propositions would have probability $\frac{1}{N}$. Ramsey does not do this, but proceeds only with fair coins. Why this restriction? Ramsey wanted everything to be based on logic, and indeed on truth functional logic. "The roulette wheel stops at 1" and "The roulette wheel stops at 2" are mutually exclusive by supposition, or perhaps by physics. Truth functional logic gives just the dichotomy "p is true," "p is false." So Ramsey can find utility $\frac{1}{2}$ in a gamble Best if Heads; Worst if Not-Heads. Finding something indifferent to this, call it Medio, he can find utility $\frac{3}{4}$ and $\frac{1}{4}$ on gambles Best if Heads, Medio if Not-Heads and Medio if Heads, Worst if Not-Heads, respectively. Utilities are squeezed by arbitrarily fine partitions. After getting the subjective utilities of everything, he can use the expected utility principle to solve for subjective probabilities of propositions that are not ethically neutral. A more detailed measurement-theoretic approach to Ramsey's theory using a bisection operator is described in Section 11.5

8
Harsanyi and Utilitarianism

After Von Neumann and Morgenstern, economists were not confined to the strict Ordinalism according to which utility levels could only be compared. They could be measured on an interval scale. But this gave no comfort for classical Utilitarianists. It is true that if everyone gives A higher utility than B on one set of individual utility scales, then after arbitrary rescalings they will continue to agree that A has higher utility than B. But if Joan prefers A and John prefers B, one choice of scales will make the Utilitarian Sum favor Joan and another will favor John. In general, the Utilitarian Sum is not meaningful for Von Neumann-Morgenstern utility. As a result, most economists dropped Utilitarianism from consideration while most philosophers, in blissful ignorance, continued to assume that utilities could just be measured like a person's weight.

But in the 1950s, a brilliant, and highly original economist, John Harsanyi, resurrected Utilitarianism on the basis of the very same Von Neumann-Morgenstern utility theory. Harsanyi, like Von Neumann and Morgenstern, was a refugee—first from the Nazis and then from the communists. Harsanyi fled with his family to Australia. He already had a doctorate in philosophy and sociology from Budapest but this was not recognized in Australia, so he took a factory job and earned an MA in economics. He then secured a job teaching at the University of Queensland. He had already published the papers we discuss here while in Australia. On a Rockefeller fellowship at Stanford, Harsanyi took a second PhD in economics with Kenneth Arrow. He spent the rest of his career at Berkeley. In 1995, he received the Nobel Memorial Prize in Economic Science.

8.1 Ideal Observer and Social Aggregation

Harsanyi's first Utilitarian paper, of 1953, used the leading idea of justice as rational decision behind a veil of ignorance, somewhat before the philosopher John Rawls (1958) used it in his famous "Justice as Fairness." Harsanyi

The Pursuit of Happiness: Philosophical and Psychological Foundations of Utility. Louis Narens and Brian Skyrms,
Oxford University Press (2020). © Louis Narens and Brian Skyrms.
DOI: 10.1093/oso/9780198856450.001.0001

was arguing that use of Von Neumann-Morgenstern utility theory was quite compatible with the use of utility in thinking about social welfare, against an influential paper that had maintained the opposite position. Harsanyi's idea was that while each individual might have her own preferences over probability distributions over social outcomes, she could also have *empathetic preferences* which result from imagining herself to be someone else. So to speak, she puts herself in someone else's shoes. Formally, she has preferences over lotteries over social outcome x, if she were individual i.

Justice is blind to special interest, so in judging the just society an individual retreats behind the veil of ignorance; she imagines that she has an equal chance of being any member of society. She gives a moral value to each social possibility using the expected value of an equiprobable gamble over being different individuals in that society.

The basic idea goes even further back to an earlier paper—then little-known—of William Vickrey[1] (1945):

> If utility is defined as that quantity the mathematical expectation of which is maximized by an individual making choices involving risk, then to maximize the aggregate of such utility over the population is equivalent to choosing that distribution of income which such an individual would select were he asked which of various variants of the economy he would like to become a member of, assuming that once he selects a given economy with a given distribution of income he has an equal chance of landing in the shoes of each member of it. Unreal as this hypothetical choice may be, it at least shows that there exists a reasonable conceptual relation between the methods used to determine utility and the uses proposed to be made of it.
>
> (p. 329)

This is a theory of justice based on rational choice behind the veil of ignorance. Rational choice means maximizing expected utility. The veil of ignorance means equal probability of being in anyone's shoes. We assume that the chooser knows Von Neumann-Morgenstern utilities for each member of society.

Now the punch line is that *if you judge justice this way, you must be a Utilitarian.* This is now called Harsanyi's "Impartial Observer Theorem." We work

---

[1] Who received the Nobel Memorial Laureate in Economic Sciences in 1996.

with a fixed population of size N. Justice utilities are expected utilities behind the veil of ignorance with equal probability of being everyone.

- Justice utility: $\frac{1}{N}U(\text{1st}) + \frac{1}{N}U(\text{2nd}) + \cdots + \frac{1}{N}U(\text{Nth})$,
- Average utility: $\frac{1}{N}[U(\text{1st}) + U(\text{2nd}) + \cdots + U(\text{Nth})]$.

For a fixed population maximizing average utility is the same as maximizing total utility. Justice is Utilitarian.

Here is an illustration. Zita contemplates two alternative social arrangements:

- (A) Monarch and nine serfs
- (B) Ten communards

Consulting her empathetic preferences, she gives being the monarch under arrangement A utility 11, and being a serf utility 1. She gives being a communard under arrangement B utility 3. Total utility under A is 20; total utility under B is 30. If you have an equal chance of being anyone, arrangement B is your best bet, with expected utility 3. Zita judges communism to be the just arrangement. That being as it may, emerging from behind the veil she prefers A, because she is the queen.

How has this argument sidestepped the roadblock of interpersonal comparison of utilities? It is simple. All these Von Neumann-Morgenstern utilities are Zita's, based on her own preferences. They are on the same scale. Her empathetic preferences over gambles on being in another's shoes do the trick.

This leads to the suspicion that the problem of interpersonal comparison may be hiding somewhere else, waiting to reappear. Suppose that Lothar approaches the same problem, with his own empathetic preferences. Lothar gives being the monarch under A utility of 21 and being a serf utility of 1. He gives being a communard under B a utility of 2. For Lothar, A is the just arrangement. Emerging from behind the veil, however, Lothar prefers B, since Lothar is a serf.

The point we are interested in here is not the very real issue of "who cares about justice?," but rather the logical point. Zita and Lothar both have a justice-as-fairness conception of justice, and both have a Utilitarian conception of justice, but they don't agree on the just society. This is not because their conceptions of justice are self-serving; we have chosen our example so that they are not. Rather it is in the logic of the argument that justice as fairness must be Utilitarian, but since utilities are personal so are judgments of social justice.

Harsanyi (1955) develops this neo-Utilitarian line of thought further. He gets the Utilitarian conclusion for group utility without "justice as fairness." The veil of ignorance and the equal probabilities of turning out to be any member of society are gone. Empathetic preferences are gone. The only moral principle linking individual and societal preferences is the Pareto principle.

This necessitates a little digression. There are various grades of Pareto principle and corresponding versions of Harsanyi's theorem. All of these link the collective preference of society to the preferences of its individual members. They represent what was left of Utilitarianism for a strict Ordinalist, which is what Pareto was. The weakest version of the principal deals only with indifference:

Weak pareto: If every member of society is indifferent between A and B, then so is society.

If one goes this far, it is plausible to extend the unanimity rule to strict inequality:

Pareto: Weak pareto + If every member of society strictly prefers A to B, then so does society.

But if everyone is to have some respect, it seems plausible to go a little further:

Strong pareto: Pareto + If some member of society strictly prefers A to B, and no member prefers B to A, the society strictly prefers A to B.

So, for example, if just one member strictly prefers A and the rest of society is indifferent, the society prefers A to B.

Harsanyi now supposes that each individual has preference orderings over lotteries of social arrangements that satisfy Von Neumann-Morgenstern axioms, and thus have corresponding Von Neumann-Morgenstern utilities. He also assumes that society—imagine an ideal social planner—should also have such coherent preferences. So society should have coherent Von Neumann-Morgenstern utilities. How should they be linked, in a Utilitarian fashion or some other way?

Harsanyi (and, following him, others[2]) show the following theorems:

1. If society's preferences satisfy Ultra-weak pareto then society's utilities are representable as a weighted sum of individual's utilities.
2. If society's preferences satisfy Weak pareto, then society's utilities are representable as a weighted sum of individual's utilities, with the weights all non-negative.
3. If society's preferences satisfy Strong pareto, then society's utilities are representable as a weighted sum of individual's utilities, with the weights all positive.

Harsanyi, in his original paper proves Theorem 1, but this allows some individuals to have a negative weight attached to their utilities. Theorem 2 precludes this, but allows some individuals to count for zero. Classical Utilitarians said that everyone counts equally, and so would certainly insist that everyone counts for something. The theorem that comes closest to classical Utilitarianism is Theorem 3.

One might object, as some have, that the weights should all be equal. But since the individuals' utilities are only unique up to choices of zero and unit, we can make each of the weights equal to 1 by choosing the appropriate units.

Theorem 3 implies:

3′ If society's preferences satisfy Strong pareto, then society's utilities are representable as a sum of individual's utilities.

This indeed is the classical Utilitarian principle. This theorem (really group of theorems) is now known as "Harsanyi's Aggregation Theorem" to distinguish it from Harsanyi's Impartial Observer Theorem.

The problem of interpersonal comparison, however, has not gone away. For example, we can reconsider Zita and Lothar, but now concentrate on their real personal preferences, not the ones behind the veil of ignorance. There are only two social alternatives, monarchy and communism. Zita prefers monarchy and Lothar prefers communism. Accordingly, on one representation of her preferences, Zita gives utility 1 to monarchy, utility 0 to communism, and utility p to a lottery between the two that gives probability p to monarchy. But we must bear in mind that these Von Neumann-

[2] See Domotor (1979) and Weymark (1994).

Morgenstern utilities are only unique up to zero and unit. Lothar has the opposite preferences. On one representation, he gives communism utility 1 and monarchy utility 0.

If we add the utilities of Zita and Lothar from the foregoing scales, we get a tie. Both monarchy and communism get a Utilitarian Sum utility of 1. Now let's transform Zita's utilities by doubling them and subtracting 1 from them. This is an equally good representation of her utilities according to Von Neumann-Morgenstern. The Utilitarian calculation then looks like this:

	Zita	Lothar	Utilitarian Sum
Monarchy	1	0	1
Communism	−1	1	0

But if we leave Zita on her original utility scale and transform Lothar's by 2x + 1, the Utilitarian Sum is 1 to 0 in favor of communism.

In fact, Harsanyi's theorem has not really constrained the Utilitarian Sum at all. This should hardly be surprising, because none of the Pareto principles apply. It is not true that all members of society are indifferent between the two options; it is not true that there is one option that each prefers; it is not true that one member is indifferent and the other has a preference. The Pareto conditions of Harsanyi's theorems are all satisfied vacuously. We are back in all the problems of intercomparability. Put another way, having a Utilitarian representation of societies does not, in itself, tell us very much. It seems quite far from Bentham.

This minimalist Utilitarianism does not seem to give us much in the way of positive social policy recommendations, although one might argue that contemporary society is Pareto suboptimal, that there are changes that could make everyone better off. On the other hand, minimal Utilitarianism seems to offer very little with which critics of Utilitarianism can take issue. One would need to object to either the assumptions of Von Neumann-Morgenstern Utility theory for society or for the individuals that make it up, or to the Pareto conditions. All these objections have been made. Individual utilities are based on individual preferences, but do individuals have coherent preferences and, if they do, do they really know what is good for them? One might consider corrected preferences, from slight corrections—which Harsanyi himself advocates—to a full-blown theory of the good.[3] Diamond

---

[3] Broome (1991), (2004).

(1967) objected to the way that expected utility treats risky prospects at the social level. Sen (1970) finds that the Pareto principle conflicts with individual rights.

Although Harsanyi's two theorems have a quite different philosophical flavor, the first depending on the veil of ignorance, and the second only on Pareto and expected utility theory, there is a connection. Notice that the impartial observer of the first theorem cannot violate Strong pareto. If arrangement A makes someone better off, and no one worst off, than arrangement B, then the ideal observer considering an equiprobable gamble between different persons, must give A higher expected utility than B.

8.2 Interpersonal Comparisons?

The previous section discussed minimal Utilitarianism, because that is all you can get from the theorems by themselves. Harsanyi, however, was not a minimal Utilitarian. He thought that interpersonal comparison of utilities was possible, and section V of Harsanyi (1955) was devoted to a searching discussion of these issues. He was well aware of the "ordinal revolution" and of accompanying skepticism regarding interpersonal comparisons, and he wanted to combat this skepticism. Here is how he opens this discussion:

> There is no doubt about the fact that people do make, or at least attempt to make, interpersonal comparisons of utility, both in the sense of comparing different persons' total satisfaction, and in the sense of comparing increments or decrements in different persons' satisfaction. The problem is only what logical basis, if any, there is for such comparisons.
>
> (p. 316)

The beginning may call to mind Russell's (1912) discussion of the problem of induction in chapter VI of *The Problems of Philosophy*:

> We have therefore to distinguish the fact that past uniformities cause expectations as to the future, from the question whether there is any reasonable ground for giving weight to such expectations after the question of their validity has been raised.
>
> (ch. VI)

We think that the similarity is intentional. Harsanyi read Russell. And Russell here is discussing skepticism. But skepticism is easy, and we must distinguish between doubts based on general skepticism and scientific doubts.

In fact, Harsanyi immediately moves to distinguish two problems of interpersonal comparison "which have not, however, been sufficiently kept apart," the metaphysical problem and the psychological problem. Harsanyi sees the metaphysical problem as just philosophical skepticism: Why should we even believe that other people have minds? Both kinds of philosophical skepticism are answered in the same way:

> If two objects or human beings show similar behavior in all their relevant aspects open to observation, the assumption of some unobservable hidden difference between them must be regarded as a completely gratuitous hypothesis and one contrary to sound scientific method.
>
> (Harsanyi 1955: 317)

In a footnote, he calls this a principle of inductive logic, and he concludes that if two people's preferences and all their outward signs of dissatisfaction are the same in any situation, we should take them to have the same utilities.

The remaining psychological problem is how to make comparisons, where people differ in these ways. Harsanyi believes that the interpersonal comparison of the magnitudes of differences in utility, which is what is needed for Utilitarianism, is an empirical question that can be addressed by scientific research. One suggestion that he had already developed in an earlier paper[4] is that one can use the fact that over time, an individual can be in different mental or physical states that affect the intensity of satisfaction experiences. This has some similarity to Parfit's observation that comparing across people is not so different from comparing present selves to past and future selves. Here, he believes that individuals can directly judge differences by introspection. A skeptic might balk here. If introspection compares remembered utility to present utility, is it to be trusted? More generally, he suggests seeing what attributions of the type under consideration play in overall explanations of individuals' behavior. A strong individual might be less averse to heavy labor than a weak one; a stronger mind might enjoy mental exercise, while a weaker one finds it painful. How this is to be spelled out

---

[4] Harsanyi (1953–4).

to give interpersonal comparability of differences is left to developments in psychology and physiology.

This not minimal Utilitarianism at all, but something closer to the classical Utilitarians. They might not be too worried about the hybridization fusing hedonic value with preference, because the fundamental principle of classical Utilitarians is that pleasure and pain govern human choices. Harsanyi's view is thus that the preferences behind Von Neumann-Morgenstern utilities are determined by hedonic differences, and that the physiological and psychological states of the individuals allow interpersonal comparisons of utility differences. Ideally, if the science were perfect, this would put all individuals on a common interval scale. In the ideal observer theorem, if the ideal observers knew the science and described the individuals to fine enough detail, then they would all agree. In the representation theorem, requiring everyone to have equal weight in the Utilitarian Sum would have a real bite.

Amartya Sen[5] (1976, 1977a) objected that Harsanyi's Utilitarianism was not classical Utilitarianism at all. This is quite true of the theorems. The theorems by themselves only give us what we have called "minimal Utilitarianism." But the theorems together with Harsanyi's view of the science of utility, can be seen as a revival of Bentham, Mill, and Edgeworth.

One may agree with Harsanyi's dismissal of the "metaphysical problem" and still question whether it gets comparability of levels and differences of utility. (Actually, all he needs for Utilitarianism is comparability of differences.[6]) If the behavior that indicates utility is choice behavior, then there is a principled difficulty. The individuals involved are assumed for the purpose of the representation theorem to be idealized expected utility maximizers. An arbitrary change of scale zero and unit for a given individual would leave that individual behaving in exactly the same way. The differences that allow comparability must be wider differences, including other psychological or neurological factors. This appears to be just what Harsanyi intends. Now the crucial comparability questions appear to depend on what these other factors are and how they themselves are measured. We will return to these questions.

---

[5] Nobel Memorial Laureate in Economic Sciences, 1998.

[6] Comparability of levels of what is needed for Rawlsian maximin or leximin social welfare evaluations. There is an extensive examination in the literature of the interaction of kinds of comparability and levels of interpersonal comparison. For a masterful treatment, see Sen (1977b).

PART II
MEASUREMENT AND PSYCHOPHYSICS

9

Neurobiology of Pleasure and Pain

9.1 Introduction

In this chapter, we give a brief discussion of the relevance of neurobiology to the measurement of utility. Modern behavioral economics has to some extent undercut the Von Neumann-Morgenstern approach by investigating cases in which individuals systematically violate each of their axioms. Some have transferred their hopes for a scientific basis for utility measurement to neurobiology. Looking at the broad outlines of established facts, we argue that this is not so. Neurobiology has all the problems that psychophysics had in constructing a hedonic scale. If anything, what we know about neurobiology of pleasure and pain just makes the problems worse.

9.2 Neurobiology of Pleasure and Pain

William Stanley Jevons was an early, if inconsistent, skeptic about the measurement of pleasure and pain. In 1871 he wrote "I hesitate to say that men will ever have the means of measuring directly the feelings of the human heart." After quoting Jevons, three leading practitioners of the new discipline of neuro-economics (Camerer et al. 2004) demur: "But Jevons was wrong. Feelings and thoughts can be measured now, because of recent breakthroughs of neuroscience." Can we now, at least in principle, build Edgeworth's hedonimeter?[1] The contemporary Utilitarian

---

[1] Edgeworth in his 1881 edition of his *Mathematical Psychics* defines the hedonimeter as follows:

> To precise the ideas, let there be granted to the science of pleasure what is granted to the science of energy; to imagine an ideally perfect instrument, a psychophysical machine, continually registering the height of pleasure experienced by an individual, exactly according to the verdict of consciousness, or rather diverging therefrom according to a *law of errors*.

The Pursuit of Happiness: Philosophical and Psychological Foundations of Utility. Louis Narens and Brian Skyrms, Oxford University Press (2020). © Louis Narens and Brian Skyrms.
DOI: 10.1093/oso/9780198856450.001.0001

philosophers Katarzyna de Lazari-Radek and Peter Singer (2014), are more circumspect: "Advances in neuroscience are making it possible for us to detect in an objective manner, whether someone is having a pleasant or a painful experience, but Edgeworth's 'hedonimeter' is still waiting to be invented." They go on to add that the problem of interpersonal comparability would remain.[2,3]

Neither thinks we are there yet. But although neurobiology is a rapidly changing field, and we do not know what the future will bring; present knowledge suggests that things will not turn out to be as simple as Edgeworth envisioned.

---

[2] De Lazari-Radek and Singer (2014: 274). See also their (2017: 70–5), where they also display a healthy skepticism about "How positive is your experience on a scale of 1 to 10" and the metric of quality of adjusted life years used on health care policy decisions.

[3] Kahneman and Krueger (2006: 5) think otherwise:

> Several methods have been used to attempt to measure the moment-to-moment flow of pleasure or pain in the laboratory. An advantage of laboratory experiments is that extraneous aspects of an experience can be controlled, and the unique effect of a stimulus on individuals' experiences can be evaluated. Participants in many experiments in psychology and in consumer research, for example, are required to undergo an experience, such as being exposed to loud noises or watching a film clip. They are asked to provide a continuous indication of the hedonic quality of their experience in real time by manipulating a lever that controls a marker on a scale, which is usually defined by extreme values such as very pleasant and very unpleasant and by a neutral value. . . .

> The participants in experiments in which a physical stimulus is varied generally provide profiles that are similar, both in level and in shape, and that respond to the stimulus in a sensible way. For example, in an experiment described in Kahneman, Fredrickson, Schreiber and Redelmeier (1993), participant ratings of pain on a 0–14 scale increased from an average of 4.0 (after the first ten seconds) to an average of 8.4 after 60 seconds of immersing their hand in water at 14° Celsius, and the average dropped to about 6.50 over the next 30 seconds, as the temperature of the water was gradually raised to 15° C.

> At the end of an experiment, individuals can be asked to evaluate their experience as a whole. Such a retrospective report can be thought of as representing the respondents' remembered utility. The evaluation of remembered utility requires the individual to remember a stream of experiences and to aggregate them in some way. Ideally, one would hope that the individual who reports his or her overall remembered utility for a period performs the task of summing momentary utilities over time that Edgeworth had in mind. This is not the case, however. Numerous studies have related individuals' retrospective evaluations of an experience to their record of real-time reports. Although retrospective evaluations are related to the real-time reports—people are generally correct in classifying a past episode as pleasant or awful—retrospective reports are also susceptible to systematic biases.

9.3 The "Pleasure Center"

In 1953, James Olds joined Donald Hebb's laboratory at the McGill University to study neurobiology of learning. Contemporary research had identified areas which when stimulated led to aversive behavior:

> Just before we began our own work, H. R. Delgado, W. W. Roberts, and N. E. Miller at Yale University had undertaken a similar study. They had located an area in the lower part of the mid-line system where stimulation caused the animal to avoid the behavior that provoked the electrical stimulus. We wished to investigate positive as well as negative effects (that is, to learn whether stimulation of some areas might be sought rather than avoided by the animal).[4]

He set out to see whether stimulation of the reticular activating system would lead to reinforcement and learning of the behavior present during the stimulation. The initial discovery was due to a lucky error:

> We were not at first concerned to hit very specific points in the brain, and, in fact, in our early tests the electrodes did not always go to the particular areas in the mid-line system at which they were aimed. Our lack of aim turned out to be a fortunate happening for us. In one animal, the electrode missed its target and landed not in the mid-brain reticular system but in a nerve pathway from the rhinencephalon. This led to an unexpected discovery.[5]

The correctly placed electrodes did not produce the desired effect, but the mistaken one did. This exciting discovery led to a program of investigating areas of the brain that had this property.

This led to 1954 path-breaking paper with Peter Milner: "Positive Reinforcement Produced by Electrical Stimulation of Septal Area and Other Regions of Rat Brain." This paper already identified more than one region involved in positive reinforcement; subsequent research expanded the list. In 1956, Olds wrote a popular account of the research in *Scientific American*, "Pleasure Centers in the Brain," and the findings became famous. Subsequent investigation describing repeated self-stimulation by rats to the exclusion of all else made for an even more powerful story.

---

[4] Olds (1956).
[5] Olds (1956).

One might think that such experiments could never be carried out in humans, but they were, in fact, carried out by Robert Heath at Tulane University in the 1970s. One infamous experiment was aimed at curing a subject of homosexuality, patient B-19. B-19 would self-stimulate by repeatedly pressing a button connected to implanted electrodes just as the rat did. Heath stimulated the patient in conjunction with heterosexual pornography. The "cure" was completed with the help of a young female prostitute recruited from the French Quarter.[6]

Some may have been tempted to think a hedonimeter is right around the corner, measuring activity in the pleasure center of the brain. There are several problems with this simplistic interpretation of Olds' experiments.

The first is that the areas that he identified as pleasure centers appear not to be pleasure centers at all. They are connected to desire rather than pleasure,

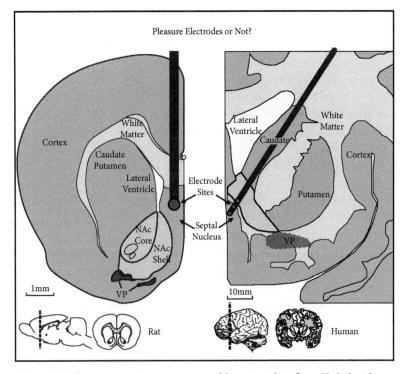

Figure 9.1 Pleasure experiment on rat and human; taken from K. S. Smith, S. V. Mahler, S. Peciña, and K. C. Berridge (2010), © OUP.

<hr>

[6] Moan and Heath (1972).

to "wanting" or incentive salience rather than "liking."[7] These centers can be blocked, and a subject can still experience pleasure. But the subject will not desire to repeat the experience. To be sure, when everything is working normally there usually is desire for pleasure, and pleasure engenders desire. But the two systems can come apart. Olds' rats and Heath's Patient B-29 kept pushing that button because the brain stimulation made them want to, not because it produced pleasure (Figure 9.1).

There are areas of the brain that are implicated in pleasurable experience, but they are not the ones that Olds discovered. Furthermore, there is not just one pleasure center, but rather many areas involved forming a complicated distributed pleasure system.

9.4 The "Pleasure Chemical"

The neurological areas that Olds investigated contained a lot of dopamine receptors. The popular meme made dopamine the neurotransmitter responsible for pleasure. With the discovery that activity in these areas did not induce pleasure, the neurological perspective shifted. The neurotransmitters primarily responsible for pleasure now appear to be endogenous opioids and cannabinoids. So, a better meme appears to be "dopamine for desire, opioids for pleasure." This, like the "pleasure center of the brain" is a gross and misleading oversimplification. As two leading neuroscientists put it:

> The idea that a brain hotspot or coding apex mediates pleasure or happiness can all too easily turn into phrenology if taken as a literal truth, and unconstrained chemo-phrenology poses an equal danger. Brain function is less constant than handy anatomical or chemical labels imply. Caveats, stipulations, and often even conditional (at least) retractions are sure to be needed, and if they are forgotten the effort to understand the brain will soon come to tears.[8]

---

[7] A similar distinction was made by the nineteenth-century Utilitarians who distinguished desire ("wanting") from satisfaction ("liking" or experiencing pleasure). This distinction continued into modern economics, where for commodities "desire" is associated with the purchase of a commodity (and measured by the price willing to be paid for it) and "satisfaction" with the pleasure produced by consuming the purchased commodity.

[8] Kringelbach and Berridge (2009).

The role of opioids alone is complex. Opioids are neurotransmitters that perform many functions in the nervous system (as does dopamine). There are opioid receptors all over the brain and, in fact, throughout the nervous system. Three different types of opioid receptors have been identified, called Mu, Delta, and Kappa. All of these are widely distributed, but frequency of different types varies with the anatomical region.

The function of these receptors in various regions of the rodent brain has been extensively investigated using various techniques, including pharmacological blockade or potentiation, and genetic knockouts.[9] The Mu receptors appear to be responsible for much of the pleasure generated by food and sex. To some extent the Delta receptors may also be involved in producing pleasure. But the Kappa receptors produce aversion. Different aspects of the opioid system are thus involved in both positive and negative reinforcement.

Rats are complicated, but humans are arguably more complicated. There are the higher pleasures, which Bentham and the Utilitarians certainly did not want to neglect. There are the pleasures of listening to music and viewing works of art, not to mention the pleasures of creating music and art for those who are so capable. There are the sympathetic pleasures of causing pleasure in others. There is evidence that these pleasures involve more of the brain than the simple sensory pleasures. They appear also to involve the neocortex,[10] although how they do so has not been extensively studied. This would not have come as a surprise to the philosopher Immanuel Kant. See his *Observations on the Feeling of the Beautiful and the Sublime*.[11] Addition neurotransmitters may come into play[12] The picture appears to be becoming more complicated.

9.5 Pleasure and Pain

Can pleasure and pain be well-represented as positive numbers on a single continuum, separated by a natural zero, in the way presupposed by Edgeworth's hedonimeter? Common experience raises caution flags. It appears to be possible to feel both pleasure and pain at the same time, as in eating food with hot peppers, or feeling the pain of intense exercise. Masochists seem to

---

[9] For a review, see Le Merrer et al. (2009).
[10] See for instance Vuurst and Kringelbach (2010: 263 ff).
[11] For an experiment inspired by, and supporting Kant, see Brielmann and Pelli (2017).
[12] Especially when we remember the full range of pleasures that Bentham considered.

cultivate the ability. This suggests that pleasure and pain should be put on different dimensions.

Some neurobiology seems to point in the opposite direction. It reveals some commonalities in pleasure and pain systems. Dopamine plays a role in anticipation of each. Opioids are involved in each kind of hedonic valence. But closer inspection reveals differences between the systems as well. Both pleasure and pain systems may be active at the same time.

The hedonimeter presupposes that a little pain cancels some pleasure; a little pleasure cancels some pain. Bentham thought that pleasure and pain interact additively, like adding positive and negative numbers. If this were so, the result would be a net hedonic value, which is what the hedonimeter would read out. Despite some analgesic effect of strong pleasure, this simple additivity picture is implausible. If the masochistic chili pepper eater prefers his pleasure with a little pain to pleasure without, he contradicts Bentham.

In a prelude discussion to their anthology, *Pleasures of the Brain*, Kringelbach and Berridge put the question directly to authors in the anthology.[13] The answers differ in interesting ways. Some say that pleasure and pain are orthogonal dimensions; others see the single dimension as a sometimes-useful heuristic.[14] None support the strict one-dimensional view in the sense discussed here.

9.6 Measurement of Pleasure in the Best-Case Scenario

Neurobiology shows that measurement of pleasure and pain in the brain is full of complications. But science marches on and sometimes it turns out that a striking simplicity lies behind complicated phenomena. At this point we would like to back away and ask what neurobiology could do for us in an idealized scenario where all the complications go away.

Suppose we consider only pleasure, and suppose that contrary to fact there is only one pleasure center of the brain and only one pleasure

---

[13] See Kringelbach and Berridge (2010: 12–13).

[14] "No. They are on orthogonal continua but usually with a mutual inhibitory relationship" (Anthony Dickenson in Kringelbach and Berridge 2010: 13); "Pain systems activate brain regions not usually included in those thought to be processing hedonic reactions and/or reward. Thus, is seems unlikely that pleasure and pain are on a continuum" (J. Wayne Aldridge in Kringelbach and Berridge 2010: 12); "In general pleasurable feelings are usually rewarding and pain is usually a punishment. There are some notable exceptions to this heuristic." (Siri Leknes in Kringelbach and Berridge 2010: 12).

chemical—call it *soma*. Suppose we can measure concentrations of soma physically, and that greater concentrations of soma correlate with reported experience of greater pleasure. In this fictional ideal case,[15] would neurobiology have solved the Utilitarian problem of the measurement of pleasure? Is pleasure then concentration of soma or square root of concentration of soma, or some other increasing function of concentration of soma? To answer this question, we must already be able to measure experienced pleasure on a scale stronger than a mere ordering. This is exactly the same problem faced by psychophysics. We have the physical measurement, but we also already need the psychological measurement to do psychophysics. Measuring pleasure with neurology presupposes an answer to the psychological measurement question. With respect to the psychological measurement, we are back in the same boat as Bentham.[16]

And further, as de Lazari-Radek and Singer remarked, it does not solve the problem of interpersonal comparison. Certainly, people are animals. If you wish, we may posit that mind supervenes on body. Ideally physically identical people in physically identical states would feel psychologically identical pleasures and pains. That alone does not tell us how to aggregate pleasures and pains in a meaningful way. The problem of interpersonal comparisons persists.

---

[15] The same considerations apply to the ideal scenario floated by Glimcher (2011).

[16] To be more explicit, suppose we have a hedonic commodity C. Amounts of C produce amounts of soma, S. C is measured physically by ϕ, and S is measured physically by σ. Let τ be the empirically determined function that maps C into S. We want the hedonimeter to describe pleasure intensity in terms JNDs. Suppose the end result is a hedonimeter scale h which results from the consumption of C. Say, for example, h is given by the JND scale,

$$h[\sigma(\tau[\phi(a)])] = k\log(\phi(a)),$$

where k is a positive constant. Such an h always exists, because any strictly increasing function (e.g., σ) can be mapped onto another strictly increasing function (e.g., $k\log(\phi)$) by a strictly increasing function (e.g., h). The issue is, How does one know that $\sigma(\tau[\phi(a)])$ is the right kind of hedonimeter scale for measuring the *subjective* intensity of the pleasure produced by a? We can only know this by being confident that some additional theory of measurement and methodology, for example Fechnerian JND measurement of C, yields $\sigma(\tau[\phi(a)])$ as the correct measure.

10

Modern Measurement

10.1 Introduction

In this chapter, we give more detail of the development of the modern theory of measurement, and the correlative concept of meaningfulness. The theory started with physical measurement of length, area, or volume, and depended on the existence of a physical notion of sameness in magnitude, and a physical addition operation such as concatenation of measuring rods. Measurement assigned numbers such that mathematical addition mirrored physical addition. This theory resulted in *ratio scales*. The account left out many measurements in the social sciences, where there was no apparent physical addition operation and no ratio scale in sight. In response psychologists introduced a range of different scales, including what we have earlier introduced as *interval scales* and *ordinal scales*. Interval scales were the type supplied for utility by Von Neumann and Morgenstern. Later a comprehensive synthesis that accounted for all these kinds of scales in terms of mirroring empirical relations was developed. The empirical relations determine scale type and meaningfulness.

From the second half of the twentieth century to present, measurement theory has made enormous advances. This book focuses on modern generalizations of (i) Herman von Helmholtz's 1887 article, "Zählen and Messen erkenntnistheoretisch betrachtet," and (ii) the theory Stanley Stevens promulgated in his 1946 *Science* article, "On the theory of scales of measurement." Generalization (i) is described in some depth in the 1971, 1990 three-volume treatise, *Foundations of Measurement* by, in various combinations of authorship, David Krantz, Duncan Luce, Patrick Suppes, and Amos Tversky. This generalization has become known as *the Representational Theory (of Measurement)*. Contemporary psychophysics has provided a generalization of (ii), which itself is founded on the Representational Theory. That generalization is discussed in Chapter 11.

The Pursuit of Happiness: Philosophical and Psychological Foundations of Utility. Louis Narens and Brian Skyrms, Oxford University Press (2020). © Louis Narens and Brian Skyrms. DOI: 10.1093/oso/9780198856450.001.0001

10.2 Extensive Measurement

Von Helmholtz was the preeminent philosopher-scientist of the second half of the nineteenth century. He made fundamental contributions to physics, physiology, and psychology that continue to have important ramifications today. His contribution to measurement theory was to formulate and give a mathematical foundation for a measurement procedure that united varied and widely used procedures of his time. He accomplished this through an axiomatic, algebraic treatment called *extensive measurement*. A key part of his method was the construction of a *standard sequence* of measurements that provided a skeleton for the assignment of numerical measurements to objects. The construction depends on a physical addition operation, $\oplus$. (For length this is linear concatenation.) For fundamental physical scales such as distance, time, mass, etc., his procedure yielded a ratio scale.

The following five steps summarize measurement through standard sequences. Proofs and some details are omitted.[1]

1. Choose a fixed object x from the domain X of objects to be the unit of measurement.
2. Construct copies of x having the same size of x by some qualitative comparison of "size"; for example, two straight physical rods x and y are of the same size, in symbols $x \sim y$, if and only if when put side-by-side their endpoints match; and x is of lesser size than y, in symbols $x \prec y$ if their left endpoints match but y's right endpoint is outside of x's, (see Figure 10.1).
3. Let $1x$ stand for x, $2x = x \oplus x$ for two copies of x, and in general $nx = (n-1)x \oplus x$ for n copies of x, n a positive integer. For any element y of X, ny is similarly defined. The sequence $1x, 2x, \ldots, nx, \ldots$, is called the *standard sequence*.
4. A function ϕ that assigns the number n to the object nx, in symbols, $\phi(nx) = n$. $\phi(nx)$ is called the *measurement* of nx, where $\phi(x) = 1$. Here measurement is reduced to counting equal sized units.

The remaining step is to assign a numerical measurement to each object y in the domain X. To accomplish this, the following assumption, called the *Archimedean Axiom*, is needed. The aim of the Archimedean Axiom is to

---

[1] A detail discussion of the method is presented in Luce et al. (1990: Vol. I, ch. 3).

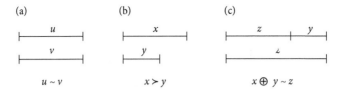

Figure 10.1 Linear concatenation of rods.

require all objects be commensurable; that is, having no object to be infinitely large or infinitesimally small in size with respect to another object. There are a number of ways to formulate this. Here we use the following: For all large positive integers k there exists a unique positive integer m_k such that $m_k x \precsim ky \prec (m_k + 1)x$. A consequence of Archimedean is that the standard sequence has the following property for each y in the domain X: For all z in X there exists p such that $z \prec py$.

5. The final part of the step shows how to measure y within an arbitrarily small fraction of the size of the unit x. By Archimedean, we know that for all large k there exists a unique positive integer m_k such that $m_k x \precsim ky \prec (m_k + 1)x$.

Define

$$\phi_k(ky) = m_k$$

to be the *approximate measurement of ky*. Then ky has been measured with respect to the unit x with error less than 1. The intuition for this is that the correct measurement of the size of ky, $\phi(ky)$, should be between measurements of the size of $m_k x$ and the size of $(m_k + 1)x$, and the approximate measurement of $\phi_k(ky)$ satisfies this, because ϕ is assumed to preserve the order $\precsim$ and

$$m_k = \phi(m_k x) \leq \phi_k(ky) \leq \phi[(m_k + 1)x] = m_k + 1.$$

Define

$$\phi_k(y) = \frac{\phi_k(ky)}{k}.$$

Then

$$\frac{m_k}{k} \le \frac{\phi_k(ky)}{k} = \phi_k(y) < \frac{m_k + 1}{k},$$

that is, $\phi_k(y)$ is an approximate measure of y with error $\frac{1}{k}$. Let

$$\phi(y) = \lim_{k \to \infty} \phi_k(y).$$

Then $\phi(y)$ is called *the measurement of y with respect to the unit x.*

The construction of the measurement function ϕ was based on the following assumptions:

1. The existence of n copies of the unit x, nx.
2. The construction of a standard sequence, $1x, 2x, 3x, \ldots$, with x as the unit.
3. The assignment of the number n as the measurement of nx.
4. The assumption of the Archimedean Axiom.

Helmholtz recognized that the length example extended to all fundamental physical dimensions, with justifications based on physical principles. Let X denote the domain under consideration. It is assumed that sizes of elements of X are compared by the empirically determined weak order $\precsim$. A binary operation $\oplus$ exists on the elements of X such that $y \oplus z$ produces another object in X. The structure $\langle X, \precsim, \oplus \rangle$ satisfies specific measurement conditions. Many of these require X, $\precsim$, and $\oplus$ to be empirically observable and satisfy empirically testable algebraic axioms about them. But two additional non-empirical axioms are necessary for the existence of representations onto an interval of real numbers. They are needed for deriving the Archimedean Axiom. The resulting axiomatic system is called *continuous extensive measurement* and it is described in Appendix 10.1.

Extensive measurement's most important axiom is *associativity*, in symbols,

$$y \oplus (w \oplus z) \sim (y \oplus w) \oplus z.$$

In relevant physical situations, associativity is testable. It is also a key characteristic of the numerical operations of addition and multiplication, that is,

$$a + (b + c) = (a + b) + c \text{ and } a \cdot (b \cdot c) = (a \cdot b) \cdot c.$$

In the presence of the other axioms, associativity allows $z \oplus w$ to be interpreted as the intensity of w added to the intensity of z.

Formally, a standard series for $\langle X, \precsim, \oplus \rangle$ is defined inductively as follows: 1 copy of x, $1x$, is x, and $n + 1$ copies of x for a positive integer n is $(nx) \oplus x$.

Hölder (1901) provided an improved and more mathematically precise version of Helmholtz's (1887) system.[2] Helmholtz's and Hölder's abstract approach to standard series provided a uniform approach for measurement in many different empirical situations that previously were unconnected. They showed the following representation theorem for extensive measurement: There exists a ratio scale of representations ϕ from X onto the positive real numbers such that for all x and y in X,

$$x \precsim y \text{ if and only if } \phi(x) \leq \phi(y) \text{ and } \phi(x \oplus y) = \phi(x) + \phi(y).$$

Extensive measurement works well for the ratio scale measurement of physical dimensions. This is because associative operations can be found or defined on them. This is not the case for psychology in general or the measurement of pleasure specifically. Consider the case of loudness. Let $\precsim$ be a weak ordering on subjective loudness. A natural psychological combining operation ∘ is simultaneously putting a sound x in the left ear and a sound y in the right ear and have the subject judge her subjective loudness $x \circ y$ for these simultaneous sounds. Empirically ∘ fails to be associative. This happens repeatedly for combining operations on subjective dimensions. In particular, ways of combining utilities subjectively fail to be associative. Thus a different form of measurement is needed for utility.

Luce and Marley (1969) generalized the idea of an extensive structure so that it need not have arbitrarily large elements. This allowed Luce (1967) to provide a qualitative axiomatic theory for probability. The idea is that one starts with a weak ordering $\precsim$ on a boolean algebra $\mathcal{B}$ of uncertain events. $A \precsim B$ stands for "B is at least as likely as A." Because disjoint unions of uncertain events correspond to the addition of probabilities, define the partial operation $\oplus$ on $\mathcal{B}$ as follows: For all A, B, and C in $\mathcal{B}$, $A \oplus B \sim C$ if and only if there exists A', B', C' in $\mathcal{B}$ such that $A \sim A'$, $B \sim B'$, $C \sim C'$, and

$$A' \cap B' = \varnothing \text{ and } A' \cup B' = C'.$$

---

[2] Also, Hölder's work on extensive measurement gave rise to his important algebraic concept of "Archimedean ordered group" by simply adding negative elements to the domain of an extensive structure.

Because the set-theoretic union operator is associative, it easily follows that $\oplus$ is associative, that is, $A \oplus (B \oplus C) = (A \oplus B) \oplus C$. Thus associativity, which is often the most difficult axiom of continuous extensive measurement to verify empirically, is here gotten for free. $\oplus$ is not defined for pairs with sums of assigned probabilities $> \frac{1}{2}$. Luce (1967) showed the following representation theorem:

Theorem 1 *There exists a unique function* $\mathbb{P}$ *from* $\mathcal{B}$ *into the real interval* *[0,1]such that for all A and B in* $\mathcal{B}$,

- $\mathbb{P}(sure\ event) = 1, \quad \mathbb{P}(\varnothing) = 0,$
- $A \precsim B$ *if and only if* $\mathbb{P}(A) \leq \mathbb{P}(B)$, *and*
- *if* $A \cap B = \varnothing$, *then* $\mathbb{P}(A \cup B) = \mathbb{P}(A) + \mathbb{P}(B)$.

The method Luce employed applies to other settings. For example, hedonic episodes, rationally considered, are similar to events in terms of structure, overlap, and disjointness. And their hedonic intensities are similar to probabilities except they are not normed to 1. This allows for a utility representation similar to Theorem 1. (A related representation of utility for hedonic events is described in Section 12.3.)

Narens and Luce (1983) describe the impact of extensive measurement on scientific measurement methods in the first half of the twentieth century as follows:

> With the successful axiomatization of extensive structures and the recognition of their importance for the foundations of physics, a curious debate ensued during the 1920s and 30s about what else is measurable. Some philosophers of physics—especially Campbell (1920, 1928) but also Bridgman (1922, 1931) and later Ellis (1966)—expounded the position that measurement from first principles is necessarily extensive in character. Campbell referred to scales resulting from such measurements as "fundamental," all else being "derived." Thus, momentum, density, and all other physical measures whose units can be expressed as products of powers of the fundamental units of mass, length, time, temperature, and charge were treated as derived. . . .
>
> At the same time, psychologists and economists were pursuing other approaches to measurement that more or less explicitly ran afoul of the dictum that fundamental measurement rests on associative, monotonic operations of combination. The debate reached its intellectual nadir with the

1940 Final Report of a Commission of the British Association for Advancement of Science (Ferguson et al. (1940)) in which a majority declared
fundamental measurement in psychology to be impossible because no
such empirical operations could be found. Campbell, a member of the
Commission, the leading figure in measurement theory at the time and
probably a major force in Commission's creation, 8 years earlier, wrote,
"Why do not psychologists accept the natural and obvious conclusion that
subjective measurements of loudness in numerical terms...are mutually
inconsistent and cannot be the basis of measurement?"

(p. 168)

10.3 Stevens' Measurement Theory

The psychologist S. S. Stevens used direct measurement techniques to measure subjective intensity. He was a member of the Commission, but failed
to convince the physicists on the Commission of the validity of the direct
measurement techniques that he employed in his psychophysical research.
His famous 1946 *Science* paper on measurement was his reply to the Commission's report. Later in 1951 he extended his ideas in an influential chapter
in his *Handbook of Experimental Psychology*. The gist of the article and
chapter was was that scale type was the important feature of measurement,
not additivity. Narens and Luce (1986) write,

> Stevens, whose work on loudness measurement with Davis in 1938 was, in
> part, at issue, was independently considering the same question in a series
> of discussions in the late 1930s with a distinguished group of scientists
> and philosophers: G. D. Birkhoff, R. Carnap, H. Feigl, C. G. Hempel,
> and G. Bergmann. Out of this arose his now widely accepted position
> that a key feature of measurement is not only the empirical structure and
> its representation, but the degree of uniqueness of the representation as
> is reflected in the group of transformations that take one representation
> into another. In contrast to Campbell, Stevens claimed that the nature
> of the transformations taking one representation onto another was the
> important feature of the representation, not the particular details of any
> axiomatization of it.
> In his 1946 and 1951 publications Stevens singled out four groups
> of transformations on the real or positive real numbers as relevant to

measurement: one-to-one, strictly monotonic increasing, affine, and similarity. And he introduced the corresponding terms of *nominal, ordinal, interval,* and *ratio* to refer to the families of homomorphisms, or scales, related by these groups.

(p. 168)

In modern measurement terms, Stevens' theory consisted of a *scale* S of functions from a domain X into the real numbers, $\mathbb{R}$. He assumed what later measurement theorists call *existence,* that is, $S \neq \varnothing$. He also assumed that the functions in S were given by some rule, but he did not put any conditions on the rule. This lead to the criticism that his very foundational idea about measurement was vague. He also assumed what later measurement theorists call *uniqueness:* there was a way of describing how any two functions in S are related to one another. This led to a classification of scales into types. Chapter 5 described the ordinal, interval, and ratio types. Here is Stevens' complete list:

Let f and g be any elements of S, and let H be such that $g(x) = H(f(x))$. Then S is said to be

- *nominal* if and only if H is one-to-one;
- *ordinal* if and only if H is strictly increasing;
- *interval* if and only if H is of the form $rx + s$ where r ranges over the positive reals and s over the reals; and
- *ratio* if and only if H is of the form rx where r ranges over the positive reals.

Later Stevens added two additional scale types:

- *absolute,* where H is the identity function, that is, S consists of a single function, and
- *log-interval,* where H is the form sx^r where r and s range over the positive reals.

There are three kinds of ratio scales S used in this book with f being an element of S: A *ratio scale,* where f is onto the positive reals, $\mathbb{R}^+$; a *ratio scale with zero,* where f is onto the non-negative reals and thus for some element z in X, $f(z) = 0$; and a *full ratio scale,* where f is onto the reals. Often the term "ratio scale" will be used to describe any of these three with context determining which is intended.

Stevens devised a direct measurement procedure for measuring subjective intensity without involving the use of an associative operation. In his procedure of *ratio magnitude estimation*, the subject is given two stimuli from the same dimension X as is asked to judge the ratio of her subjective intensities for them. These ratios are used to produce a function from X onto the reals, which is taken to be a representative of the scale that measures the subject's subjective intensities for elements of X. Stevens assumed that this scale was a ratio scale, presumably because the subject was asked to judge ratios. To many scientists this last assumption made no sense. Narens and Luce (1983) says the following about it:

> The method, which he [Stevens] dubbed "magnitude estimation," has been moderately widely used because it produces quite systematic results. Nevertheless, it has proved extremely difficult to defend his assumption that the method of magnitude estimation actually results in ratio scales. Although he recognized more than anyone else at the time the significance of scale type in contrast to the particular structures exhibiting it, he seemed not to appreciate that, in fact, the concept of scale type is a theoretical one that can only be formulated precisely in terms of an explicit axiomatic model of an empirical process. He failed to acknowledge that it takes more than one's intuitions to establish that a measurement process, such as magnitude estimation, leads to a ratio scale.

Having characterized scales by the type of transformation involved, Stevens went on to emphasize that scientific and statistical propositions formulated in terms of measured values must exhibit invariance of meaning under the admissible transformations that characterized the scale type. He called such invariant propositions *meaningful*. As pointed out before, there are two scale types for temperature used in science: An interval scale used before the establishment of absolute zero that has the Farenheit and Centigrade as representations, and a ratio scale with zero that has the Kelvin representation that came after the establishment of absolute zero temperature. More empirical structure corresponds to smaller classes of transformations that preserve it. For temperature an example is that $\frac{°5}{°4}$ is meaningful when temperature is measured in degrees Kelvin but not meaningful when measured in degrees Centigrade.

10.4 Representational Theory of Measurement

The Representational Theory of Measurement, or *Representational Theory* for short, combines, in a general setting, ideas from the classical theory based on extensive measurement with those from Stevens. Its methods have the same rigorous scientific standards as the classical theory, but emphasize Stevens' approach to scale types and meaningfulness. It is based on approaches suggested by Scott and Suppes (1958) and Suppes and Zinnes (1963). Scott and Suppes write,

> A primary aim of measurement is to provide a means of convenient computation. Practical control or prediction of empirical phenomena requires that unified, widely applicable methods of analyzing the important relationships between the phenomena be developed. Imbedding the discovered relations in various numerical relational systems is the most important such unifying method that has yet been found.
>
> (pp. 116–17)

The kind of imbeddings they employ are homomorphisms.[3] The Scott-Suppes theory had no meaningfulness concept. This was remedied by Suppes and Zinnes (1963) who extended the theory to include Stevens' meaningfulness concept.

The Representational Theory generalizes the main ideas behind extensive measurement. In extensive measurement axioms in terms of an empirically observable operation, $\oplus$, and an empirical observable relation, $\precsim$, are given where the axioms are testable by experiment, except for one used to derive the Archimedean Axiom. In the Representational Theory, the operations and relations of the qualitative structure remain observable but they are

---

[3] Recall function φ from the domain X of the qualitative structure

$$\langle X, R_1(x_1, \ldots, x_n), \ldots, R_k(y_1, \ldots, y_m) \rangle$$

into the domain $D \subseteq \mathbb{R}$ of the numerical structure

$$\langle D, S_1(w_1, \ldots, w_n), \ldots, S_k(z_1, \ldots, z_m) \rangle$$

is said to be a *homomorphism* if and only if for all $x_1, \ldots, x_n$ and $y_1, \ldots, y_m$ in X,

$$R_1(x_1, \ldots, x_n) \text{ if and only if } S_1[\varphi(x_1), \ldots, \varphi(x_n)]$$

$$\vdots$$

$$R_k(y_1, \ldots, y_m) \text{ if and only if } S_k[\varphi(y_1), \ldots, \varphi(y_m)].$$

not otherwise restricted. Axioms in terms of these are given, and in most applications the critical ones lead to experimental testing. An example of this is the conjoint measurement of loudness in terms of the intensity and frequency of pure tones.

Let the Cartesian product $I \times F$ denote the set of pure tones if having intensity i and frequency f. Let $if \precsim jg$ if and only if jg is perceived as being at least as loud as if. Then psychophysicists are interested in knowing if they can measure $I \times F$ in the following manner: There exists functions ψ on I and θ on F such that for all if and jg in $I \times F$,

$$if \precsim jg \text{ iff } \psi(i) + \theta(f) \leq \psi(j) + \theta(g). \qquad 10.1$$

In this case, the additivity of the loudness dimension is expressed by the psychological interaction physical intensity and frequency. The issue is, How to characterize this in terms of observations about $\precsim$? Measurement theorists investigated this and eventually worked out systems where Equation 10.1 holds. They called their systems *additive conjoint measurement* and showed the following uniqueness theorem: If ψ and θ are elements of interval scales on, respectively, I and F, and if ψ' and θ' are any two functions satisfying Equation 10.1 then there exist real numbers r, s, and t with $r > 0$ such that

$$\psi' = r\psi + s \text{ and } \theta' = r\theta + t. \qquad 10.2$$

Note that in Equation 10.2 the same real number r is used as a multiplicative term in the characterization of ψ' and θ' and that the additive terms s and t can be different.

A key axiom in additive conjoint measurement is the Thomsen Condition defined below. It is a conjoint way of saying "associativity," but it takes some mathematical calculation to make this apparent.[4]

Thomsen Condition: $\precsim$ is said to satisfy the Thomsen Condition if and only if for all i, j, and k in I and all f, g, and h in F,

If $if \sim jg$ and $jp \sim kf$, then $ip \sim kg$.

---

[4] See Krantz, et al. (1971: ch. 6) for a full discussion of this and other properties involved in additive conjoint measurement.

10.5 Scale Type

Let S be a scale from X onto R $(= \mathbb{R}$ or $\mathbb{R}^+)$.

Then S is said to be *order preserving* if and only if $\leq$ is meaningful, that is, for all x and y in X and φ and ψ in S,

$$\varphi(x) \leq \varphi(y) \text{ if and only if } \psi(x) \leq \psi(y).$$

Stevens considered six types of scales: absolute, ratio, interval, log-interval, and nominal. Of these, all but nominal are order preserving, of the five order preserving ones, the interval-scale and log-interval-scale types are really variants of each other rather than fundamentally different scale types. They are related by a logarithmic transformation,

$$sf^r \rightarrow r\log(f) + \log(s);$$

This makes them have different but isomorphic *transformation groups*, that is, they have different but isomorphic forms of uniqueness. This is why we call the log-interval-scale type a "variant" of an interval scale rather than a fundamentally new scale type. That leaves four of Stevens' ordered scale types without variants: absolute, ratio, interval, ordinal.

Three of these, absolute, ratio, and interval are *finitely unique* in the sense that if two representations φ and ψ agree on n distinct values for some nonnegative integer n, then $\varphi = \psi$. Ordinal scales are not finitely unique. Ratio, interval, and ordinal scales are *homogeneous* in the following sense: For each r in R and each φ in S there exists x in X such that $\varphi(x) = r$. Absolute scales are not homogeneous.

So far, it has been ratio and interval scales that have been the most important for science. This leave open the question in Stevens' classification: Are there additional scale types that are homogeneous and finitely unique that may be of importance for science?

Narens (1981) and Alper (1987) investigated this and showed that for homogeneous finitely unique order-preserving scales there existed only additional scale types between ratio scales and interval scales.[5] Luce and Narens (1985) provided arguments that the only ones of these that are

---

[5] See Luce et al. (1990: ch. 20) for a discussion and proof.

likely to have application in science are the log discrete interval scales with transformation groups on $\mathbb{R}^+$ of the form,

$$\text{log discrete interval: } y \to k^n + s,$$

where k is fixed and positive, n ranges over the integers, and s ranges over the reals. Thus Stevens was close to listing all scale types that were likely to have major applications in mathematical science. He did not, however, provide theoretical assurance for this.

The Representational Theory derives the scale type of the measurement of an empirical situation from axiomatic assumptions about its underlying empirical structure. The most important assumptions—those seen as the driving force in deriving the representation and uniqueness theorems—were designed to be able to be checked empirically. Narens (1981) and Narens and Luce (1986) recognized that *one-point uniqueness*, where any two representations agree for an object had to be identical, could be established for many kinds of situations without making strong structural assumptions like associativity or the Thomsen Condition. Luce and Narens (1985) went further showed that two-point uniqueness, where any two representations agree for two distinct objects had to be identical, held for many kinds of qualitative or empirical situations. By the above results of Narens and Alper, this suggests that if homogeneity could also be established, then the only possible scale types that are to lead to situations having "laws" and strong mathematical structure are ratio, log discrete interval, interval, or transformed variants of them. Narens (1981) and Luce and Narens (1985) provided methods for empirically testing homogeneity, but such tests are difficult to carry out. A different approach is to assume that one of the three homogeneous scale types holds. The following provides a rationale for this approach.

Let S be a scale of one of the three homogeneous finitely unique scale types. Then $S \neq \varnothing$. So let φ be in S. Then the image $\varphi(R)$ for each relation of the qualitative structure $\mathfrak{R}$ is a numerical relation, and these images can be used to construct a numerically representative structure $\mathfrak{N}$ for S. Suppose S is an interval scale. Then each of these images are invariant under the transformations in S. This puts a huge restriction on the mathematical form of $\mathfrak{N}$. This restriction provides insights on how to test the theory or, put differently, how to add testable assumptions about $\mathfrak{N}$. After considering S to be an interval scale, the process is repeated by considering S to be a discrete log interval scale and, after that, considering S to be a ratio scale. This leads to three different theories to be postulated and tested. This approach has been successfully carried out by Luce (2000) for developing theory and analyzing data for utility theories based on gambles.

10.6 Modern Measurement: Concluding Remarks

During the nineteenth-century, the only scientific way to measure pleasure was through Fechner's method of JND. Some, for example Eddington, considered it as a central part of Utilitarianism. However, this was only for theory. Little experimentation was done, with Wundt's psychophysical measurement of pleasure being the notable exception. The twentieth century brought forth a plethora of new measurement techniques. Most could be conceptualized as applications of the Representational Theory. These included measurement methods prior to the founding of the Representational Theory, for example, the utility theories of Ramsey and of Von Neumann and Morgenstern.

Stevens' methods of measurement, which were based on subjective veridical interpretations of numbers, don't fit into the Representational Theory. They were taken by scientists and philosophers to lack an adequate foundation. But, as will be shown in Section 11.4, they too can be conceptualized within the Representational Theory if the interpretations of numbers are not taken to be veridical. When this is done and experimental comparisons to Stevens' theory are made, Stevens' theory is found wanting.

In the Representational Theory, the choice of the numerical representing structure is arbitrary. Different representing structures will produce different numerical expressions for the representation of qualitative or empirical relations and statements. But this does not cause a problem, if isomorphisms are used for representations and attention is paid to meaningful relations and sentences.[6]

---

[6] Suppose $\mathfrak{R}$ and $\mathfrak{S}$ are representing structures for the qualitative structure $\mathfrak{Q}$, ϕ and ψ are respectively representations of $\mathfrak{Q}$ onto $\mathfrak{R}$ and $\mathfrak{S}$, and $\mathfrak{R}$ and $\mathfrak{S}$ are measured by scales of isomorphisms, and T is a statement about $\mathfrak{Q}$ formulated in terms of the primitive relations of $\mathfrak{Q}$. It is known from logic that isomorphisms preserve truth. Thus,

$$T \text{ iff } \phi(T) \text{ iff } \psi(T). \qquad 10.3$$

Equation 10.3 holds for all representations ϕ and ψ of $\mathfrak{Q}$. Thus each statement about $\mathfrak{Q}$ formulated in the language about $\mathfrak{Q}$ has the same truth value and is meaningful in any isomorphic numerical representing structure. This implies the meaningless propositions of $\mathfrak{R}$ and $\mathfrak{S}$ are exactly those that cannot be formulated in terms of the primitive relations of $\mathfrak{Q}$.

Scale types are important measurement considerations. Many laws essentially reduce to relations between scale types.[7] Knowing that the scale types onto the continuum that are of interest to science are restricted to ordinal, interval, ratio, and absolute, with one between interval and ordinal that has not been used, put Luce's program and substantial generalizations of it on an intellectually sounder foundation.[8]

Appendix 10.1. Definition of Extensive Structure

Let X be a non-empty set, $\precsim$ be a binary relation on X, and $\oplus$ is a binary operation of X. We write $x \prec y$ if $x \precsim y$ and not $y \precsim x$. Then $\mathfrak{X} = \langle X, \precsim, \oplus \rangle$ is said to be a *continuous extensive structure* if and only if the following seven axioms hold for all x, y, and z in X.

- *Weak Ordering*: $\precsim$ is a reflexive and transitive ordering on X.
- *Density*: If $x \prec z$ then for some w in X, $x \prec w \prec z$.
- *Associativity*: $\oplus$ is *associative*; that is,

$$(x \oplus y) \oplus z = x \oplus (y \oplus z).$$

- *Monotonicity*:

  $x \precsim y$ if and only if $x \oplus z \precsim y \oplus z$ if and only if $z \oplus x \precsim z \oplus y$.

- *Solvability*: For all x and y in X, if $x \prec y$, then for some w in X, $x \oplus w = y$.
- *Positivity*: $x \prec x \oplus y$ and $y \prec x \oplus y$.
- *Continuous Domain*: There exists a function f from X onto $\mathbb{R}^+$ such that

  $x \precsim y$ if and only if $f(x) \le f(y)$.

The following theorem of Helmholtz and Hölder characterizes extensive measurement as a form of ratio scale measurement:

Theorem 2 *Suppose $\mathfrak{X} = \langle X, \precsim, \oplus \rangle$ is a continuous extensive structure. Then the set $\mathcal{S}$ of representations (homomorphisms) of $\mathfrak{X}$ onto $\langle \mathbb{R}^+, \le, + \rangle$ is a ratio scale.*

---

[7] This was first noticed by R. Duncan Luce (1959) in his seminal article, "On the Possible Psychophysical Laws."

[8] For theory and examples, see Falmagne and Narens (1983) and Falmagne and Doble (2015).

11

Psychophysical Measures of Intensity

11.1 Introduction

Modern psychophysics has advanced our understanding of the Utilitarian issues raised in the nineteenth century. Some of the conundrums associated with JND are solved by Luce and Narens by showing how they can arise from continuous latent variables. A rigorous mathematical analysis of measurement by the alternative means of bisection is now available. It is nice to find this technique at the heart of Frank Ramsey's treatment of probability before the general modern theory was available. There are, however, problems that remain. For instance, there is the problem of multimodal comparisons by a single individual. The mathematical prerequisites for putting different modalities on a single scale are now well understood, but the relevant empirical tests are few and sometimes fail. Experiments of this kind for the different modalities of pleasure and pain are missing. Are things likely to be simpler here than in the case of loudness? Doubtful. Some psychophysical experiments seem to indicate the subjects cannot distinguish ratios from differences. Problems remain.

Three measurement procedures for collecting psychophysical data are discussed in this chapter: (i) JNDs, (ii) making mid-point judgments, and (iii) giving a number that describes the intensity of a stimulus or the ratio of two stimuli intensities or their difference. How the numbers in (iii) are applied is up to the investigator. They are utilized in widely different ways, from constructing a scale using only their ordering to one using the proffered numbers as their scale values. This raises the issue of the agreement of methods. Psychophysicists take this issue very seriously. Their answer is "Roughly." An outsider might take this as "good enough," considering the high level of precision of good psychophysical experimentation. But for psychophysicists "roughly" is not good enough and they argue for one method over another.

The literature on the measurement of pleasure and pain rarely uses, by current standards, rigorous psychophysical methods. Instead, methods that were discredited by the nineteenth-century scientific community are still

The Pursuit of Happiness: Philosophical and Psychological Foundations of Utility. Louis Narens and Brian Skyrms, Oxford University Press (2020). © Louis Narens and Brian Skyrms.
DOI: 10.1093/oso/9780198856450.001.0001

in use. Much of it is beyond sloppy; it is meaningless: for example rating scales of happiness where the ratings are averaged. Many philosophers and social and medical decision makers base their theories and decisions on these studies. It is the purpose of this chapter to show that serious thought has been put into the measurement of subjective intensities by psychophysicists; their theory and methods are general and likely applicable to the measurement of the subjective intensities of pleasure and pain.

11.2 Semiorders and Just Noticeable Differences

11.2.1 Comparison of Just Noticeable Differences and Standard Sequences

A sequence of 1 JND, 2 JND, 3 JND, . . . resembles a standard sequence $1x$, $2x$, $3x$, . . . from extensive measurement. They can be used to measure things, JNDs with a constant error and standard sequences with arbitrarily small error. There appears to be some similarity in Fechner's and others treatments of them in that they are conceived of as being "equally spaced." However, the assignment of 1 to 1 JND, 2 to 2 JND, 3 to 3 JND, will turn out to be by the Representational Theory a convention, just like the assignment of the number n in extensive measurement to n copies of the unit x. One could equally well declare that the JND spacing should be such that each "space" is twice its previous "space," that is, $1\,\mathrm{JND} = 1$, $2\,\mathrm{JND} = 2$, $3\,\mathrm{JND} = 4, \ldots, n\,\mathrm{JND} = 2^{(n-1)}, \ldots$. Then in terms of physical measurement, the sequence would look like a version of Weber's Law with Weber's constant $c = 1$.

11.2.2 Luce's Axiomatization

Fechner had an empirical approach to JND measurement. Luce (1956) provided a representational approach. He defined an ordering $x \prec y$ on stimuli meant to capture the idea that y was at least 1 JND more than x in subjective intensity. He gave axioms about $\prec$ with each corresponding to a simple experiment. He showed that if his axioms held in a setting consisting of finitely many stimuli, then there was a numerical representation Ψ on the stimuli such that

$$x \prec y \text{ if and only if } \Psi(x) + 1 \leq \Psi(y),$$

that is, the psychological intensity $\Psi(y)$ of y is at least 1 JND (+1) more intense than the psychological intensity $\Psi(x)$ of x. Luce's axioms were about finite situations. Narens (1994) extended the theory so that it applied to a continuum of stimuli. The following is an equivalent of Luce's axioms.

$\prec$ is said to be a *semiorder* if and only if X is a non-empty set, $\prec$ is a binary relation on X, and the following three axioms are true for all w, x, y, and z in X:

1. Not $x \prec x$.
2. If $w \prec x$ and $y \prec z$, then $w \prec z$ or $y \prec x$.
3. If $w \prec x$ and $x \prec y$, then $w \prec z$ or $z \prec y$.

We will interpret $y \prec x$ as x is more discriminably intense than y.

There are many kinds of empirical semiorders. Fechner's experimental paradigm provides an example. There the semiorder $x \prec_p y$ is defined by the observed frequency, p, of y being subjectively more intense than x is $\geq p$. Taking $p = .75$ gives one semiorder; $p = .9$ another.

Luce's semiorder axioms are testable by refutation. For example, 2 is refutable by finding *particular* w, x, y, and z such that

$$w \prec x \text{ and } y \prec z,$$

but not

$$w \prec z \text{ or } y \prec x.$$

Thus Luce's axiomatic approach provides a simple method of testing for the failure JND modeling. Note that this is radically different than the usual procedures of statistical model testing through goodness of fit. It is more sensitive for rejecting models.

An important property of semiorders is that a subject can be indifferent to stimuli without indifference being an equivalence relation.

Define $\sim$ on X as follows. For all x and y in X,

$$x \sim y \text{ if and only if } x \nprec y \text{ and } y \nprec x.$$

If $x \sim y$, we say x is *indifferent* to y. Then, except for degenerate cases, $\sim$ is *not* an equivalence relation, that is, generally there are x, y, and z in X such that $x \sim y$, $y \sim z$, but not $z \sim x$.

As an example, define $\prec$ on $\{.5, 1.3, 2, 2.4\}$ by $x \prec y$ iff $y - x > 1$. Then $1.3 \sim 2$ and $2 \sim 2.4$, but $1.3 \nsim 2.4$. But note that although $\prec$ does not distinguish 1.3 and 2 by a direct comparison, they can be compared *indirectly*: 2.4 is obviously discriminably larger 1.3, because 2.4 is discriminably more intense that 1.3 but only indifferent to 2. This idea leads to a way to weakly order the domain of a semiorder using the following definition.

Let $\prec$ be a semiorder on X. Define $\precsim_*$ as follows: For all x and y in X,

$$x \precsim_* y \text{ if and only if for all } z, \text{ (if } y \prec z \text{ then } x \prec z) \text{ and (if } z \prec x \text{ then } z \prec y).$$

Luce (1956) showed that $\precsim_*$ is a weak order, that is, it is a transitive and connected relation. $\precsim_*$ is appropriately called the *weak order induced by* $\prec$. Luce (1956) also showed the following theorem.

Theorem 3 *(Luce's representation theorem) Suppose X is a finite set of stimuli and $\prec$ is a semiorder on X. Then there exists a function Ψ from X into the real numbers such that for all x and y in X,*

$$x \prec y \text{ if and only if } \Psi(x) + 1 < \Psi(y).$$

Say for real numbers $r < s$ that s is 1 JND more than r if and only if $r + 1 = s$. Then, by Luce's theorem, $x \prec y$ if and only if the measurement $\Psi(y)$ of y is at least 1 JND more than the measurement of x, $\Psi(x)$.

While experiments are about finite sets of stimuli X, most of economic and psychophysical theory are about infinite X on a Weakly Ordered Continuum. Unfortunately the method of proof of the Luce's representation theorem does not extend to a continuum of stimuli. (See Appendix 11.1 for a formal definition of "continuum.") Narens (1994) came up with a different method for this situation.

Suppose $\langle X, \prec \rangle$ is a semiorder. Then $\langle X, \prec \rangle$ is said to be *continuous* if and only if $\langle X, \precsim_* \rangle$ is a continuum.

Theorem 4 *Suppose $\langle X, \prec \rangle$ is a continuous semiorder and $\precsim_*$ is the weak order induced by $\prec$. Define the binary relation T on X as follows. For all x and y in X, $T(x) = y$ if and only if for all z in X,*

(i) *if* $y <_\star z$ *then* $x < z$, *and*
(ii) *if* $z <_\star y$ *then* $x \nprec z$.

Then T is a function on X and has the property that for each x in X,

$$x < T(x).$$

T is called the *threshold function induced by* $<$. It has the characteristic property that for each x, if (i) $T(x) \lesssim_\star T(y)$ if and only if $x \lesssim_\star y$, and (ii) if $T(x) <_\star y$ then $x < y$.

Narens (1994) showed the following JND representation theorem, where $T(x)$ is 1 JND greater than x.

Theorem 5 *(Continuous Semiorder Theorem) Suppose* $\langle X, < \rangle$ *is a continuous semiorder with induced ordering* $\lesssim_*$ *and induced threshold function T. Then there exists a function* Ψ *from X onto* $\mathbb{R}$ *such that for all x and y in X,*

$$x \lesssim_* y \ \ \text{if and only if} \ \ \Psi(x) \leq \Psi(y)$$
$$\Psi[T(x)] = \Psi(x) + 1.$$

In psychophysics, stimuli from X are presented to the subject. A semiorder is computed from the subjects' responses. It belongs to the subject and is considered psychological. The stimuli, however, have both psychological and physical roles. Its physical role, if relevant, is not part of the psychological structure $\langle X, < \rangle$ but is part of a different structure used to measure physical stimuli. Throughout this section it will be assume that this physical structure is the weakly ordered extensive structure $\mathfrak{X}_\oplus = \langle X, \lesssim', \oplus \rangle$. Other ratio scalable physical structures can be used to measure X, but it is convenient to stick with $\mathfrak{X}_\oplus$. Psychophysics proceeds by relating the psychological and physical structures. There are many ways to do this. Two are considered in this section.

The first is the method suggested by Fechner and used by most psychophysicist and measurement theorists. This method links physical measurements of a stimuli to its psychological measurement through a psychophysical function. Additional assumptions are made and tested about this function so its mathematical form can be described. The other, suggested by Narens and Mausfeld (1989) is to put the psychological and physical structures into a single structure and make additional assumptions involving only relations from these structures. No psychophysical function is posited. It is derived. The Narens and Mausfeld approach make very clear in what manner the structures are compatible. It is used in the axiomatizations of the rest of this chapter. The two approaches are discussed again in Section 11.7.

Consider the psychophysical structure $\langle X, \precsim', \oplus, \prec \rangle$. Its part, $\langle X, \precsim', \oplus \rangle$ is the physical structure with axioms saying it is an extensive structure, and its part, $\langle X, \prec \rangle$, is the psychological structure with axioms saying it is a semiorder. An additional axiom, $\precsim' = \precsim_*$, is added where $\precsim_*$ is the $\prec$-induced weak ordering. This axiom expresses the psychophysical law that the subject's behavior orders stimuli in exactly the same manner as in physics. Notice that this is testable.

Formulating a qualitative equivalence to Weber's Law is slightly more complicated. It is that for all x and y in X,

$$T(x \oplus y) = T(x) \oplus T(y), \qquad\qquad 11.1$$

were T is $\prec$'s induced threshold function. It is also testable. It provides an alternative to the traditional method of verifying if and where Weber's Law holds.

Section 4.5 presented Von Kries' criticism of Fechner's method for establishing JND measurement of sensation is based on convention. Leaving most of the discussion of "convention" aside until Section 11.7, the main point to be made here contrary to Von Kries is that JND measurement *done through semiorders* is just as foundationally rigorous as extensive measurement of physical qualities. The axioms of semiorders are few, simple, and are universally quantified statements. Although Von Kries may be correct in his attack on Fechner's and others' interpretation of JND measurement, it should be noted that this attack, appropriately reformulated as in Section 11.7, works just as well on physical measurement as used by psychophysicists.

11.3 Bisection Measurement

Fechner considered direct measurement of sensation as unscientific. For Plateau's study of the psychophysical function of grays, this amounted to whether the midpoint grays produced by his artist subjects were really the mid-points on their subjective scale of grayness. In other words, *Did Plateau's subjects carryout the instructions correctly?* Plateau did not provide an argument for them doing so. In terms of modern measurement theory, Fechner was correct in that Plateau's study had serious scientific flaws. But Fechner was wrong in thinking that they couldn't be corrected: Plateau only needed to collect the right kind of bisection data to determine whether his artists carried out correctly the bisection instruction.

What does such data consist of? It is the non-refutability of the relevant axioms given below of a continuous bisection structure. The observed failure of any one of these axioms would show that the subjects were not carrying out the instructions correctly. The holding of the axioms show that the bisection structure $\mathfrak{X} = \langle X, \precsim, \textcircled{1} \rangle$ is isomorphic to $\langle \mathbb{R}, \leq, \oplus \rangle$, where $r \oplus s = \frac{1}{2}(r + s)$, and thus it is consistent with true bisection taking place in $\mathfrak{X}$. To show this, we start by defining what bisection is qualitatively. $x \textcircled{1} y$ is read as *the bisection of x and y*. We apply bisection to provide a different proof of Ramsey's utility theory. Gambles by repeated flips of an unbiased coin provides a paradigmatic case of Ramsey's theory. Bisymmetry, defined below, is a generalization bisection. It allows for Ramsey to be generalized to repeated flips a biased coin, although we won't do it here.

$\langle X, \precsim, \textcircled{1} \rangle$ is said to be a *continuous bisection structure with bisection operation* $\textcircled{1}$ if and only if $\textcircled{1}$ is a binary operation on X and the following seven conditions axioms for all w, x, y, and z in X:

1. *Weakly Ordered Continuum*: $\langle X, \precsim \rangle$ is a Weakly Ordered Continuum.
2. *Idempotence*: $w \textcircled{1} w \sim w$.
3. *Intern*: If $x \prec y$ then $x \prec x \textcircled{1} y \prec y$.
4. *Solvability*: There exist u and v in X such that $u \textcircled{1} x \sim v \textcircled{1} y$.
5. *Monotonicity*: $x \prec y$ if and only if $x \textcircled{1} z \prec y \textcircled{1} z$, and $x \sim y$ if and only if $x \textcircled{1} z \sim y \textcircled{1} z$.
6. *Commutativity*: $x \textcircled{1} y \sim y \textcircled{1} x$.
7. *Bisymmetry*: $(w \textcircled{1} x) \textcircled{1} (y \textcircled{1} z) \sim (w \textcircled{1} y) \textcircled{1} (x \textcircled{1} z)$. (Bisymmetry is illustrated in Figure 11.1.)

Theorem 6 *Suppose* $\mathfrak{X} = \langle X, \precsim, \textcircled{1} \rangle$ *is a continuous bisection structure. Then* $\mathfrak{X}$ *and* $\mathfrak{N} = \langle \mathbb{R}, \leq, \oplus \rangle$ *are isomorphic, where* $\oplus$ *is the binary operation on* $\mathbb{R}$ *such that for all r and s in* $\mathbb{R}$

$$r \oplus s = \frac{1}{2}(r + s).$$

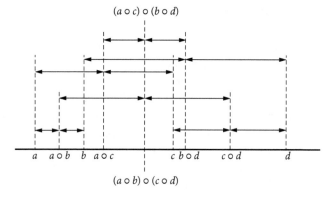

Figure 11.1 The figure illustrates the special case where commutativity also holds, $a \circ b = b \circ a$, etc., making $\circ$ a bisection operation.

Proof. Theorem 10 of section 6.9 of Krantz et al. (1971) and theorem 2.1 of Luce and Narens (1985).[1]

11.4 Making Magnitude Production Indirect

The nineteenth-century Utilitarians and economists considered the direct measurement of pleasure to be untrustworthy beyond supplying ordinal rankings. So did twentieth- and twenty-first-century economists, many in psychology—particularly psychophysicists—as well as researchers involved in the foundations of science. Nevertheless, direct measurement remains a primary tool today for measuring well-being, often through rating scales employing statistical analyses computed through non-ordinal statistics requiring the data to be measured on a ratio or an interval scale. Foundational justifications, if given at all, tend to rely on Stevens' theory or ideas similar to it.

---

[1] The first four axioms of theorem 10 of section 6.9 of Krantz et al. (1971) easily follow from the Conditions 1 to 7. The remaining axiom (the Archimedean Axiom) follows from Theorem 2.1 of Luce and Narens (1985).

Stevens' method of magnitude production—where a subject is asked for a stimulus x and positive number p to find a stimulus y that is experienced as being "p-times as intense than x"—is a convenient tool for obtaining data about subjective intensity. Stevens thought that using this kind of data to measure y as the measurement of x multiplied by p led to a ratio scale having the same scientific legitimacy as those found in science, for example in physics. He and others generated a massive psychophysical literature showing that his direct methods produce interesting, applicable, and reproducible results. Fechner would have disdained these methods, and many in psychophysics today also find them unscientific, despite their empirical validity and usefulness. The theme of this section is that Stevens, and colleagues, conclusions about the the psychophysical law being a power function follows from the kind of data they collected, but if proper measurement-theoretic foundations are employed, a different and empirically more accurate law will result—often a power law with a different exponent.

This section follows ideas of Narens (1996) that take magnitude production *data* of the same sort used by Stevens, but use it through a representational theory approach to produce an indirect method that yields a ratio scale. It is expected, and is shown in a case involving model comparison, that the representational theory approach provides a better fit to data.

Stevens' rules for assigning numbers to magnitude productions are clear. What is not clear, however, is what else is needed to produce a rigorous algebraic account of what is being assume by his magnitude production procedure for it to yield a ratio scale. Narens (1996) develops a theory for this.

He first isolates two principles that he believes are inherent in Stevens' direct methods of measurement. Although these principles are not stated explicitly by Stevens, they, according to Narens, are implied by,

  (i) his data collection methods,
  (ii) his methods of statistical analysis, and
  (iii) the conclusions he drew from his experimental research.

Let S be the scale resulting from magnitude production using Stevens' method.

Principle 1: S is a ratio scale family that adequately measures the observer's subjective intensity of stimuli in X.

Stevens' apparently believed that a ratio scale resulted because the subjects are estimating ratios. While results of this section suggest that this is the case, there is, however, a big difference between (i) guessing a correct result and justifying it through word-play, and (ii) justifying it through an accepted mathematical-empirical theory.

Principal 2: For each t in X, there is a function ψ_t in S such that (i) $\psi_t(t) = 1$, and (ii) for each x in X, if the subject's behavior is that she produces x as the response to "p-times t," then $\psi_t(x) = p$.

Theorem 8 below shows that Principles 1 and 2 imply the "Multiplicative Property" defined below. Empirical results discussed later show the the Multiplicative Property fails for human judgments for standard psychophysical stimuli. Narens (1996) diagnosed the problem being in Principle 2, which is at the heart of Stevens' method of magnitude production. The following clarifying notation is helpful for explaining why.

Throughout the rest of this section, the following notation is used for all t and x in X and positive integers p: $f_p(t) = x$ if and only if x is the subject's response to "Find the stimulus x that is p-times in intensity to stimulus t." f_p is called a *magnitude production function*. Note that in terms of ψ_t in Principles 1 and 2,

$$f_p(t) = x \text{ if and only if } \psi_t(x) = p. \qquad 11.2$$

For some purposes the notation "f_p" is more revealing, and for others the notation "ψ_t" is more revealing.

Definition 7 *Multiplicative Property:* For all for t in X and all positive integers p and q,

$$f_q[f_p(t)] = f_{q \cdot p}(t).$$

The Multiplicative Property is easy to check in the data, if appropriate data has been collected to decide it. It says that for $p = 2$ and $q = 3$ that producing two times the subjective magnitude of t followed by three times that magnitude should be the same as producing six times that magnitude. Tests like this weren't done by Stevens and the psychophysics community until relatively recently. And, as described below, the $p = 2$, $q = 3$ test fails dramatically. This causes serious foundational problems for Stevens' theory, because of the following theorem:

Theorem 8 *Suppose S is a scale of representations from X onto $\mathbb{R}^+$ satisfying Principles 1 and 2. Then the Multiplicative Property holds.*

The proof of Theorem 8 is given in Appendix 11.

Consider the following example that tests the Multiplicative Property: A sound x is produced that is perceived as twice as loud as t, and the sound y that is perceived as three times as loud x, should yield a sound z that is perceived as six times as loud as t. Empirical results of Ellermeier and Faulhammer (2000) and others show that such z are produced that are perceived as being more like twelve times as loud, as opposed to six. This is a very large discrepancy. Zimmer (2005) found similar results using $\frac{1}{2}$, $\frac{1}{3}$, $\frac{1}{6}$, and $\frac{1}{12}$. Experimental tests of the Multiplicative Property has been tested many times in several sensory domains by several laboratories. In particular, it fails for loudness and brightness.[2]

Narens (1996) predicted that the Multiplicative Property would likely fail. He suggested it be replaced by a weaker principle for evaluating magnitude production that he called the "Commutativity Property." It is implied by the Multiplicative Property.

Commutativity Property: For all for t in X, and all positive integers p, q,

$$f_q[f_p(t)] = f_p[f_q(t)].$$

For $p = 2$ and $q = 3$, the Commutativity Property says that for a stimulus t, the response to produce "2 times t" followed by "3 times t" is the same as "3 times t" followed by "2 times t."

Narens (1996) showed the following theorem.

Theorem 9 *Assume Commutativity Property. Then there exists a ratio scale S of representations on X and a function W from $\mathbb{R}^+$ onto $\mathbb{R}^+$ such that for all x in X, positive integers p, and φ in S,*

$$\varphi[f_p(x)] = W(p) \cdot \varphi(x). \qquad 11.3$$

---

[2] See Luce et al. (2010) for references.

When $W(p) = p$, Equation 11.3 reduces to Stevens method magnitude production.

Call $\langle X, \precsim, f_p \rangle_{p \in I^+}$ a *magnitude production structure,* where $\langle X, \precsim \rangle$ is a Weakly Ordered Continuum and the f_p are magnitude production functions. Narens (1996) gave an indirect measurement account of magnitude production structures that resulted in Equation 11.3 with $W(p) = p$. This produces the same result from magnitude production data that one would obtain using Stevens' method of measurement. But Narens' version did not use Stevens' method. He used the Representational Theory. Most of his assumptions were simple, obvious ordinal ones, for example, $t \precsim f_p(t)$, or assumptions necessary for mapping onto the positive real numbers. The following three are the main ones in need of empirical justification:

(1) For all t in X, $f_1(t) = t$.
(2) The Multiplicative Property.
(3) The Commutativity Property.

The theorem that results with (1) and (2) is that *there exists a ratio scale S such that Equation* 11.3 *holds with* $W(p) = p$. Narens also showed that the replacement of the Multiplicative Property with the Commutativity Property then yields the more general theorem, *there exists a ratio scale S such that Equation* 11.3 *holds.*

When explicitly tested for, (1) fails in some loudness experiments.[3] However, it holds in brightness experiments. The apparent reason for the failure in loudness is that the two stimuli must be given successively for evaluation. In brightness, they can be presented simultaneously. A model comparison test involving distance and area judgments was conducted in Bernasconia et al. (2008), involving Equation 11.3 and Stevens' method. Both statistically fit the data. Equation 11.3 provided a better fit than Stevens' method.[4] (2), the Multiplicative Property, generally fails, but the Commutativity Property generally holds.[5]

---

[3] Steingrimsson and Luce (2012).
[4] They also tested a more complicated psychophysical model of Luce (2004) that predicted commutativity on the same data and found its fit couldn't be distinguished from Narens but was better than Stevens. (This model of Luce's is briefly described in Section 11.8.)
[5] See Luce et al. (2010).

11.5 Ramsey's Utility Theory Revisited

Utilitarianism measures pleasure with utility functions. Its literature and more recent developments—for example, Von Neumann-Morgenstern—have provided a variety of ideas for doing this. This section looks at using bisection structures from the Representational Theory of Measurement (Section 11.3) for this purpose. When accompanied by ideas employed by Ramsey in Section 7.2, this volume, a rational theory is produced. In order to carry this out in detail, a formal structure and some formal definitions are needed.

Let E be an Ethically Neutral Event in the sense of Ramsey (e.g., a flip of a fair coin),[6] $\bar{E}$ its complement, X_0 be a set of pleasurable stimuli, $\precsim$ a weak ordering that orders X_0 by pleasurableness, and u be a utility function that preserves $\precsim$.

For x and y in X_0, let (x, E, y) be the gamble of receiving x if E occurs and y if $\bar{E}$ occurs, that is, E doesn't occur. Such gambles based on ethically neutral events E and ranging over all x and y in X_0 are called *(neutral) gambling operators*. Intuitively, $u(x, E, y)$ should be half-way between $u(x)$ and $u(y)$; that is, the gambling operator (x, E, y) should correspond to a bisection operator $\oplus$ on $\langle X, \precsim \rangle$. "Half-way" here means that the subject is indifferent between (x, E, y) and $(x, \bar{E}y)$. This is what is behind Ramsey's utility theory for binary outcome ethically neutral gambles. However, bisection measurement theory was not around at Ramsey's time, and he had to invent his own version of it.

Three measurement theories for utility that use the idea of bisection will be developed and compared:

(i) A utility theory using bisection and Stevens' philosophy.
(ii) A utility theory based on standard experimental methods using the representational theory.
(iii) A rational interval-scale utility theory in the spirit of Ramsey using the representational bisection measurement.

Stevens' method, (i), proceeds by fixing $x \prec y$ and assigning numbers to x and y, say 1 to x and 2 to y. These numbers fix a utility function. (They can be changed to any pair of number p and q as $p < q$ with x being assign

---

[6] The definition of an Ethically Neutral Event is provided later.

to p and y to q.) The subject is asked to find the mid-point between x and y. Say she picks z. Then the experimenter assigns 1.5 to z, the number that is mid-point between 1 and 2. The experimenter then asks the subject to find the mid-point between z and y and assigns 1.75 to it. The experimenter asks the subject to find the w such that x is the mid-point between w and z, and assigns .5 to w. By continuing in this manner the experimenter can produce a measuring function that measures each pleasure in X_0 within an arbitrarily small error. Note that in (i), data is collected in a manner so that all that is needed to be checked is the bisection choice was between the presented pleasures to be bisected with respect to $\prec$. From this it is apparently concluded or assumed that the subject understood the instruction to bisect and produced a theoretically appropriate response.

Representational bisection theory, (ii), proceeds somewhat in the same manner as (i), except there are more rigorous tests for saying, "The subject carried out bisection in an appropriate manner." These consist of also testing the measurement theoretic axioms for bisection and commutativity. Section 11.3 presents an exact description of the Representational Theory's axiomatization of bisection. A subject can succeed in matching the criteria for doing bisection in (i) but fail in (ii), for example, by meeting all the axioms for a bisection structure except for the axiom of bisymmetry,

$$(x \oplus y) \oplus (z \oplus w) \sim (x \oplus z) \oplus (y \oplus w),$$

or the axiom of commutativity,

$$x \oplus y \sim y \oplus x.$$

The theory behind (ii) correctly captures the semantics of "bisection" as far as is possible for concepts formulated in terms of X_0, $\precsim$, and $\oplus$. This is because Theorem 6 says $\langle X, \precsim, \oplus \rangle$ is isomorphic to $\langle \mathbb{R}, \leq, \oplus \rangle$, where $r \oplus s = \frac{1}{2}(r+s)$. In other words, (ii) captures the correct behavior according to the correct semantics of "bisection" relative to $\precsim$ and $\oplus$, whereas (i) only captures part of it. The act of bisecting can further be specified and tested by providing additional concepts to the setup. This was for Ramsey here by the inclusion of neutral gambling operators.

We will assume for a rational agent for which all neutral gambling operators with outcomes in X_0 produce identical bisections, and that these bisections are the same as the bisections produced by $\oplus$ described in (ii). This, as an assumption of rationality, has been questioned and argued about in the literature, with Ellsberg (1961) proposing counterexamples. Because this section is only concerned with *hedonic utility* and not *decision utility*, we can be very selective in the kinds Ethically Neutral Events to be considered. In particular we need not compare what Ellsberg would call *ambiguous* Ethically Neutral Events, for example, a flip of a coin coming up heads of which we have no knowledge whether or not it is biased, with an *unambiguous* neutral ethical event, for example, a flip of a known fair coin coming up heads. So we will assume that all the Ethically Neutral Events to be considered are unambiguous and avoid the potential difficulties raised by Ellsberg. Then Appendix 11.3 presents a bisection version of Ramsey's theory for two-outcome esthetically neutral events.

11.6 Torgerson's Conjecture

Torgerson (1961) used data from his own experiments and others to conclude that at some fundamental level experimental subjects do not distinguish ratios from differences:

> Several years ago, Garner (1954) tried to get subjects first to set a variable stimulus between two standard stimuli so that the successive differences were equal, and second, to set the variable so that the successive ratios were equal. That is, first, so that $V-S_1 = S_2-V$, and second, so that $V/S_1 = S_2/V$. For most of his subjects—thirteen out of eighteen—the value set for the variable was the same in the two conditions: Equal subjective intervals were also equal subjective ratios....
>
> These results are all consistent with the notion that the subject perceives only a single quantitative relation between stimuli. When this relation is interpreted as either a psychological distance or a psychological ratio, it can be shown that the subjective magnitudes obey the properties of the corresponding commutative group—the addition group for the distance interpretation and the multiplication group the ratio interpretation.
>
> (pp. 204–5)[7]

---

[7] A similar observation about the necessity of comparing pairs when measuring value was made the nineteenth-century Utilitarian philosopher Samuel Baily. It was based on the exchangeability of economic commodities instead of psychology:

> As we cannot speak of the distance of any object without implying some other object between which and the former this relation exists, so we cannot speak of the value of a commodity, but in reference to another commodity compared with it. A thing

Torgerson's conclusion is often called Torgerson's Conjecture. There are many experiments supporting it and some contradicting it. Many of the supporting studies are based on direct measurement techniques, raising issues about their validity. These are resolved by developing indirect approaches. For example, Birnbaum and Mellers (1978) observed that if subjective ratios and differences were qualitatively the same, as suggested by Torgerson, then they had to be ordered the same manner. In particular,

$$D(a, b) < D(c, d) \text{ iff } R(a, b) < R(c, d), \qquad 11.4$$

where $D(x, y)$ is the judged numerical difference between x and y, $R(x, y)$ their judge numerical ratio. Thus if Equation 11.4 holds, direct measurement, which takes the size of these numbers to correctly correspond to a veridical scale of subjective intensity, cannot be valid, for example, $2 - 1 < 10 - 8$ but $\frac{10}{8} < \frac{2}{1}$.

The failure of direct measurement is not surprising. It has been suspicious as a measurement technique from the beginning of experimental psychology. But the holding of Equation 11.4—a consequence of Torgerson's Conjecture—is nevertheless surprising. Why should direct measurement fail in such a way to yield the strong law expressed by Equation 11.4?

There have been many very carefully performed studies—several with seasoned, sophisticated, psychophysical subjects—that demonstrated the Conjecture. There are also some that show the Conjecture is wrong. In any case, this literature should make one pause about accepting conclusions requiring difference judgments necessarily be interpreted as differences or ratio judgments definitely interpreted as ratios. Birnbaum (1990) writes,

> Torgerson (1961) theorized that the dispute between Stevens' law [the Power Law] and Fechner's[the logarithm law] was a dispute over theory, not data. Data that would support Fechner's law under the subtractive interpretation would support Stevens' law under the ratio interpretation. Torgerson's argument went further: if subjects only perceive a single relation between stimuli despite variations in the task, then the choice between the subtractive and the ratio theory (and therefore between Fechner and Stevens) would be a decision, not an empirical discovery.

(p. 50)

cannot be valuable in itself without reference to another thing, any more than a thing can be distant in itself without reference to another thing.

Baily (1825: 5)

11.7 Representation as a Convention

11.7.1 Alternative physical measurement

Section 4.5 presented Von Kries's view about the choice of unit for JND measurement, where Von Kries took the position that measuring by a representation having equal JNDs did not follow from empirical facts. It was a convention. The Representational Theory of Measurement takes a similar position: The choice of the numerical representing structure is arbitrary. This choice is up to the theorist and is made for convenience or for some reason external to the measurement process. Any numerical structure isomorphic to the chosen numerical structure would do just as well.

As an example, consider the measurement of length. Figure 11.2 shows the essential qualitative relationships for the the continuous extensive structure $\mathfrak{X} = \langle X, \precsim, \oplus \rangle$, for measuring length. Here X is the set of measuring rods and $\oplus$ is the operation of concatenating rods by abutting one to another in a linear order. It turns out that for classical physics, fundamental physical attributes like length can be appropriately measured by different continuous extensive structures on the same attribute. Although such measurement yields different ratio scales on the same physical attribute, it does not in any serious way affect the quantitative aspects of physics. Krantz, et al. (1971) wrote the following about this:

> As Ellis (1966) pointed out, at least one other totally different interpretation of concatenation also satisfies the axioms [for a continuous extensive structure on lengths] and so leads to an additive representation; this measure of length is not linearly related to the usual one. Campbell (pp. 290–294 of 1957 edition) discussed other examples of a similar nature.
>
> To present Ellis' interpretation we begin with a collection of rods. Let [the concatenation] $a * b$ be the hypotenuse of the right triangle whose

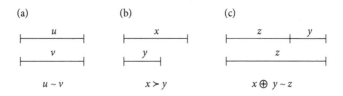

Figure 11.2 Linear concatenation of rods.

sides are a and b. The comparison relation $\succsim$ is determined by placing two rods side by side, with one end coinciding, and observing which one extends at the other end [(a) and (b) in (Figure 11.2)]. Using properties of right triangles it is easy to verify that [the axioms of a continuous extensive structure] are satisfied. The only property that might present a slight difficulty is associativity. It is explained in (Figure 11.3) where the lines are labeled by their lengths in the usual measure. Since [the axioms of a continuous extensive structure are] satisfied, [an additive representation results], hence there is a measure ψ that is order preserving and additive over this new concatenation. Since the usual measure ϕ is also order preserving, ψ and ϕ must be monotonically related, and by the properties of triangles it is easy to see that ψ is proportional to ϕ^2.

To most people, the new interpretation seems much more artificial than the original one. In spite of this strong feeling, neither Ellis nor the authors know of any argument for favoring the first interpretation except familiarity, convention, and, perhaps, convenience. We are used to length being measured along straight lines, not along the hypotenuses of right triangles, but no empirical reasons appear to force that choice. Indeed, we could easily reconstruct the whole of physics in terms of ψ by replacing all occurrences of ϕ by $\psi^{\frac{1}{2}}$. This would make some equations appear slightly more complicated; others would be simpler. In fact, when ϕ^2 happens to be the more convenient measure, it is common to assign it a name and to treat it as the fundamental measure. Examples are the moment of inertia and the variance of a random variable. In the present case, if a and b are rods, the squares with side a and with side b can be concatenated by forming the square on the hypotenuse; ϕ^2 will be an additive (area) measure for such concatenation of squares.

(Krantz et al. 1971: 87–8)

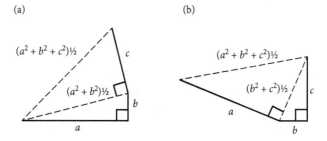

Figure 11.3 (a) Orthogonal concatenation for length measurement and (b) illustration of the associativity property.

This idea generalizes to other dimensions and powers. It is based on the following foundational idea from an area of physics know as "dimensional analysis": All physical dimensions are products of powers of a small number of basis dimensions. For example, momentum, mv, is the product of basis dimensions of mass, m, and velocity, v; energy, mv^2, the product of basis dimension mass, m, and the square of the basis dimension velocity, v^2, etc. The principle that there are many physically equivalent ways of measuring each physical dimension follows from the fact that the continuous extensive structure used to measure each basis dimension through an additive representation φ has, for each power $s \geq 1$, an alternative continuous extensive structure with the same domain and additive representation θ such that $\theta = \varphi^s$.[8] This fact about alternative continuous extensive structures and powers of additive representations that are used in the next section.

11.7.2 The Equivalence Principle

Fechner characterized psychophysics as a form of duality that had a physical structure of stimuli and a psychological structure of sensations. These existed independently of one another. Psychophysics then proceeded by describing the function that related the physical measurements of stimuli to the psychological measurements of the sensations they engendered. Qualitatively, this is represented as a single structure,

$$\mathfrak{F} = \langle X \cup Y, X, P_1, \ldots, P_n, Y, R_1, R_m, F\rangle,$$

where $\langle X, P_1, \ldots, P_n\rangle$ is the structure used to measure the physical stimuli, $\langle Y, R_1, R_m\rangle$ is the structure used to measure the the psychological sensations, and F is a one-to-one function from X onto Y. While this captures how psychophysics is generally formulated, it violates the dualism that keeps psychology and physics separate, because the psychophysical function F belongs neither to the psychology nor the physics.

Narens and Mausfeld (1992) models matters so that F is not a primitive relation. Instead, it is a function whose existence and proprieties are derivable from from assumptions that are formulated in terms of relations that are about purely physical matters or purely psychological matters. They change the formulation of psychophysical structure to the following:

---

[8] See Narens and Mausfeld (1992) for a discussions.

$$\mathfrak{X} = \langle X, P_1, \ldots, P_n, R_1, \ldots, R_m \rangle$$

is a psychophysical structure with substructures $X_\Phi = \langle X, P_1, \ldots, P_n \rangle$ for measuring the physical situation and $X_\Psi = \langle X, R_1, \ldots, R_m \rangle$ for measuring the psychological responses to presentations of stimuli from X. They call this kind of psychophysical structure *separable*. In the separable case, the set of physical stimuli X is common to both structures. In X_Φ they are regular physical objects undergoing physical measurement; in X_Ψ they are psychological stimuli presented for psychological intensity evaluation. The R_i are psychological relationships on psychological stimuli. They are behavioral objects. Their phenomenology only enter in through theory, if they are interpreted—as Fechner would want them to be—as being an isomorphism of relations on sensations induced by the presence of physical stimuli. This phenomenological interpretation isn't needed for doing psychophysics, and most modern studies eschew it.

Separable representations make clear what is being assumed in terms of purely physical and purely psychological relations. These relations are sometimes combined in a statement stating a psychophysical law. Weber's Law provides an example.

Consider the psychophysical structure $\mathfrak{X} = \langle X, \leq_1, \oplus, \precsim \rangle$, with physical continuous extensive structure $X_\Phi = \langle X, \precsim_1, \oplus \rangle$ and psychological continuous semiorder $X_\Psi = \langle X, \prec \rangle$. Let $\precsim_*$ and T respectively be the weak ordering induced by $\prec$, and let T be $\precsim$'s threshold function. Let ϕ be an additive representation for X_Φ and ψ be a JND representation for X_Ψ. Then the following theorem holds.

Theorem 10 *The following three statements are logically equivalent:*

1. *Weber's Law: There exists $c > 0$ such that for all x in X,*

$$\frac{\phi[T(x)] - \phi(x)}{\phi(x)} = c.$$

2. $\precsim_1 = \precsim_*$ *and* $\psi(x \oplus y) = \psi(x) \oplus \psi(y)$.
3. $\psi = \log \phi$.

Note that Statement 2 of Theorem 10 uses only primitives from $\mathfrak{X}_\phi$ and $\mathfrak{X}_\psi$ and a JND representation of $\mathfrak{X}_\psi$.

Theorem 10 does not depend on the physical structure used to measure X. It only depends on

(i) X being the domain of *any* continuous extensive structure,

(ii) X being weakly ordered by identical physical and psychological relations, and

(iii) the JND representation ψ and the physical concatenation operation $\oplus$ satisfy $\psi(x \oplus y) = \psi(x) \oplus \psi(y)$.

Thus any continuous extensive structure satisfying (i)–(iii) will produce the same result in Theorem 10 for $\mathfrak{X}_\psi$. This makes Weber's Law a law about the physics of the situation and not just a "law" that depends a particular way—among many ways—of measuring the physical situation. Narens and Mausfeld (1992) call the generalization of this idea to separable psychophysical situations the *Equivalence Principle*. It causes difficulties for some kinds of conclusions psychophysicists draw about Weber constants or exponents of power laws in cross-modal situations.[9] For example, one cannot say that for a particular subject, modality 1 has greater sensitivity to smaller differences in stimulation than modality 2, because the Weber constant for modality 1 is smaller than the Weber constant for modality 2, This is because the size of Weber's constant depends on which alternative physical continuous structure is being used to measure the stimulus.

11.8 Cross-Modality Measurement

The above example of Weber constants illustrates the difficulty inherent in comparing different psychophysical dimensions in terms of dimension-less constants. Additional structure beyond the constants is needed. One

---

[9] Narens and Mausfeld (1992: 475) comment,

It should be noted that although most psychophysical researchers have ignored the potential problems involved in the choice of scale of the physical variable in deter-mining psychophysical power functions, a few (e.g., Krueger, 1991; Myers, 1982; Weiss, 1981, 1989), have directly commented on this issue and noted that because of it, many kinds of psychophysical comparisons across modalities are not properly founded. Our methods for reaching similar conclusions are different, are more rigorously founded in theory, and are base exclusively on how the psychological and the physical are related using the Equivalence Principle.

type of additional structure used by psychophysicists is to have subjects make direct comparisons of subjective intensities across dimensions. This is like the Utilitarian issue of comparing different kinds of pleasures. Intra-comparability issues like these can be formulated in a number of ways. This section uses the following formulation of Narens (2006): *When can two scales of a given type of an underlying continuum be combined into a single scale of the same type?* This way of formulating matters transforms what is often stated as somewhat obscure problem into a well-defined mathematical one.

Recall the following quote from Edgeworth's from his 1881 *Mathematical Psychics* that maintains utility can be measured in a single dimension of intensity × time:

> Utility, as Professor Jevons says, has two dimensions, intensity and time. The unit in each dimension is the just perceivable [Wundt, *Physiological Psychology*] increment. The implied equation to each other of each *minimum sensible* is a first principle incapable of proof. It resembles the equation to each other of undistinguishable events or cases [Laplace, *Essai–Probabilities, p. 7*] which constitutes the first principle of the mathematical calculus of *belief.* It is doubtless a principle acquired in the course of evolution. The implied equatability of time intensity units, irrespective of distance in time and kind of pleasure, is still imperfectly evolved. Such is the unit of *economical* calculus.
>
> (p. 7)

Edgeworth employed equal JND measurement as a method for measuring pleasure. The method was well-thought of in nineteenth-century psychology and is still in use for constructing psychophysical scales. Von Kries objection to equality of JNDs having the same size still holds. So far, the empirical research on the matter is consistent with Edgeworth's position that the equality of JNDs is incapable of proof. Some, however, consider it an empirical matter. For example, in a review of psychophysical research Teghtsoonian (2012) writes the following about cross-modal equal JNDs:

> What is being assumed is that a JND defined on one of those [physical] continua will be matched by a JND on the other. Indeed, it is an empirical question that, to my knowledge, has yet to be tested.
>
> (p. 170)

Edgeworth also assumed the commensurablity of JNDs between people on the same and different dimensions and that people had different capacities for pleasure.

In order to make ideas about commensurability clear, let's formulate matters mathematically so that we can carry out deductions that may not be obvious in ordinary language—that is, prove theorems about commensurability.

We start with the case where Persons 1 and 2 are on the same weakly ordered physical continuum of stimuli, $\langle X, \precsim_{\Phi} \rangle$. We suppose they have, respectively, continuous semiorders $\prec_1$ and $\prec_2$ giving rise to induced orderings and threshold functions on X, $\precsim_{*,1}$, $\precsim_{*,2}$, T_1, and T_2, respectively. It is assumed that the psychophysical law,

$$\precsim_{\Phi} = \precsim_{*,1} = \precsim_{*,2},$$

holds. The issue then becomes: *Under what conditions does a joint JND representation ψ for $\prec_1$ and $\prec_2$ exist? That is, When does there exist ψ is such that for all x and y in X,*

$$x \prec_1 y \text{ if and only if } \psi(x) + 1 < \psi(y),$$

and for some positive r,

$$x \prec_2 y \text{ if and only if } \psi(x) + r < \psi(y)?$$

This is strictly a mathematical question.

Narens (1994) provided the following necessary and sufficient answer: *When T_1 and T_2 commute, that is, when for all x in X,*

$$T_1[T_2(x)] = T_2[T_1(x)]. \tag{11.5}$$

Equation 11.5 is easy to test. If it holds then $\prec_1$ and $\prec_2$ have a common representation ψ representing the JNDs for $\prec_1$ so they are 1 apart and representing the JNDs for $\prec_2$ so they are r apart.

Without loss of generality, suppose $1 \leq r$. For Edgeworth, if x for Person 1 is approximated at n JNDs—making her utility for comparison purposes n for x—then for Person 2, x is approximated at $\frac{r}{n}$—making his utility $\frac{r}{n}$ for x. (The case of $r < 1$ is handled in the same way.) Thus, if commutativity holds, then the same utilities result as those calculated using Edgeworth's JND representations. But in this case, commutativity, which is a principle that is capable of verification or refutation, is assume instead of Edgeworth's "incapable of proof" Axiom.

If instead of commutativity, the stronger condition that both Persons 1 and 2 semiorders satisfy Weber's Law (which implies commutativity by a simple calculation) is assumed, then the same result about intercomparability resulting from commutativity holds.

The above case is about the comparability of JNDs of two individuals on a single dimension of stimuli. What about two on two dimensions? There are various kinds comparisons:

(1) A single agent comparing intensities on two dimensions of physical stimuli. This is called an *intrapersonal comparison*.

(2) An agent comparing her subjective values of pleasure with another agent's subjective values of pleasure. This is called an *interpersonal comparison*.

(3) An external agent (e.g., a social planner) making the comparison.

(2) and (3) have no counterpart in psychophysics, but are central considerations in ethics. Psychophysics achieves equivalents of (1) through cross-modality judgments.[10]

The Utilitarians from Bentham onward were aware of the difficulty of the measurement issues involved in the cardinal comparisons of the sizes of different kinds pleasures. Some thought that because they can be ordinally compared, they could be put on the same scale and thus their cardinal measurement would, theoretically, require nothing different than in the

---

[10] The following is an example by Luce et al. (2010) that does this through magnitude productions:

Narens (1994, 1996, 2006) describes how ratio scalability is equivalent to various Commutativity Properties. In particular, Narens (2006) suggests a method for showing how separate ratio scales can be combined into a single ratio scale by way of Commutativity Properties. Luce et al. (2010) and Steingrimsson et al. (2012) carried out experiments testing this idea for comparing loudness of different tones and brightness of different colors. They found that each tone had its own ratio scale for loudness and that these could be compared through cross-modal magnitude judgments, that is, judgments like, "Find the tone in dimension 2 that is twice as loud as this tone from dimension 1." They found their qualitative commutativity conditions to hold, which is mathematically equivalent to the existence of a common ratio scale for both dimensions of tones, and they found similar results held for brightness of different colors. However, there were subtleties that raised serious coherence concerns. These and a summary of their methods and results are given in Appendix 11.4.

measurement of a single kind of pleasure. But, as the Luce et al. (2010) and Steingrimsson et al. (2012) showed, this view is too simplistic.

11.9 Intrapersonal Psychophysical and Utility Aggregation

Bentham and the Utilitarians thought that different pleasures experienced by an individual could be combined to produce an aggregate pleasure. They took the utility of this aggregate to be the sum of the utilities of the individual pleasures. However, they did not provide a sound justification for this or any other form of aggregation. As discussed earlier, related issues occur in psychophysics; for example, aggregating the loudness of tones from different frequencies into a single loudness measure, or the the brightness of different colored lights into a single brightness measure. Individual utility aggregation is discussed in Appendix 11.5. It assumes the existence of a common scale for the aggregate and its dimensions. The following issue is its focus: *How do meaningfulness considerations limit the mathematical form of the aggregating function.* This is looked at for the case of the aggregation of two utility functions from a single person. Similar ideas and methods will apply to psychophysical stimuli as well to the aggregation involving more dimensions. Chapters 12 and 13 consider utility aggregations across different people.

11.10 Psychophysical Measures: Concluding Remark

This chapter presented some of the psychophysical measurement techniques used in modern psychophysics. The measurement theory behind them is now well-understood. Bentham would have liked to see rigorous measurement applied to all kinds of pleasure and pain. He would have liked to know whether these measurements then agreed, to provide a robust scientific concept. We have to say that most of this program of empirical psychophysics remains to be carried out.[11]

---

[11] One small exception. In the 1960s, Ekman carried out experiments where two different measurement techniques were used, and then the relationship between the results were analyzed. The methods were essentially direct ratio estimation, and a sophisticated version of JND measurement. One experiment measured moral repugnancy of various scenarios; others measured degrees of beauty. Ekman found the scale from one kind of measurement agreed with

In contrast, many contemporary studies of pleasure and pain, happiness and well-being just blast away, get some numbers, and treat them as if they had some absolute meaning. Issues of measurement and meaningfulness seem to be forgotten. "What is this pain on a scale of 1 to 10?", "How pleasant is this on a scale of 1 to 10?" just don't cut it. We can do better.

Appendix 11.1. Cantor's Continuum Axiomatization

Quantitatively, a continuum is a finite or infinite interval of real numbers. It the domain of most models in mathematical science. Its qualitative, foundational properties were laid out in Cantor (1895). The following is a version of Cantor's treatment for a weak ordering without endpoints.

Definition 11 (continuum) $\langle X, \precsim \rangle$ is said to be a *Weakly Ordered Continuum* if and only if the following four statements hold:

1. *Weak Ordering*: $\precsim$ is a weak ordering on X.
2. *Unboundedness*: $\langle X, \precsim \rangle$ has no $\precsim$-greatest or $\precsim$-least element.
3. *Denumerable Density*: There exists a denumerable subset[12] Y of X such that for each x and z in X, if $x \prec z$ then there exists y in Y such that $x \prec y$ and $y \prec z$.
4. *Dedekind Completeness*: $\langle X, \precsim \rangle$ Dedekind complete.[13]

Theorem 12 (Cantor's Continuum Theorem) $\mathfrak{X} = \langle X, \precsim \rangle$ *is a Weakly Ordered Continuum if and only if there is a function φ from X onto $\mathbb{R}^+$ such that for all x and y in X,*

$$x \precsim y \text{ if and only if } \varphi(x) \leq \varphi(y).$$

Proof.   Cantor (1895). (A proof is also given in theorem 2.2.2 of Narens 1985.)

This theorem is true if $\mathbb{R}^+$ is replaced by any interval of reals without endpoints, including $\mathbb{R}$. It is an immediate consequence of Theorem 12

---

the log of the scale from the other. This supports Torgerson's Conjecture that was discussed in this chapter.

[12] That is, a subset Y that is in one-to-one correspondence with the positive integers.
[13] That is, each $\precsim$-bounded nonempty subset of X has a smallest $\precsim$ upper bound.

that the set of representations from $\mathcal{X}$ onto $\langle \mathbb{R}^+, \leq \rangle$—or, equivalently, onto $\langle \mathbb{R}, \leq \rangle$—is an ordinal scale.

As customary in psychophysics and utility theory, unless explicitly stated otherwise, we will assume and model ideal cases where stimuli are on a continuum.

Appendix 11.2. Derivation of the Multiplicative Property

Proof. Let $\psi_t(x) = p$, $\psi_x(y) = q$, and $\psi_t(y) = r$. By Principles 1 and 2, let s be a positive real such that

$$\psi_x = s \cdot \psi_t.$$

Then

$$1 = \psi_x(x) = s \cdot \psi_t(x) = s \cdot p$$

that is,

$$s = \frac{1}{p}.$$

Thus,

$$q = \psi_x(y) = s \cdot \psi_t(y) = \frac{1}{p} \cdot \psi_t(y) = \frac{1}{p} \cdot r,$$

in other words, $r = p \cdot q$. In terms of f_p and f_q this yields,

$$f_q[f_p(t)] = f_{q \cdot p}(t).$$

Appendix 11.3. Ramsey's Theory

Throughout this section, let A and B be probabilistically independent ethically neutral events. As previously,

- X_0 is a set of pleasurable stimuli.

The goal is to construct an interval-scale utility function on X_0 using a bisection measurement so that the utility of the gambles (x, A, y) and (x, B, y) are the bisections of the utilities of x and the utilities of y. To do this, we need additional concepts. The first extends the notion of "gamble of pleasures" to include "gambles of gambles of pleasures": Let

- X_1 be $X_0 \cup$ the set of gambles of the form (x, A, y) and (x, B, y), where x and y are in X_0;
- X be the set of gambles of the form (x, A, y) and (x, B, y), where x and y are in X_1; and
- $\precsim$ be a binary relation on X.

$x \precsim y$ is interpreted as before as "y gives at least as much pleasure to the agent as x."

The following axiom is assumed about $\precsim$:

- *Weakly Ordered Continuum*: $\langle X, \precsim \rangle$ is a Weakly Ordered Continuum.

This assumption of Weakly Ordered Continuum simplifies the statement of the needed representation and uniqueness theorem. It can be weakened to produce a more general result.

The next two axioms follow from the above and the definition of "ethically neutral" and the fact that the complement of an Ethically Neutral Events is ethically neutral.

Suppose A and B are ethically neutral. Then for all x and y in X,

- *Insensitivity Across Ethically Neutral Events*: $(x, A, y) \sim (x, B, y)$.
- *Ethically Neutral Complement*: A is ethically neutral if and only if $\bar{A}$ is.

We assume a rational agent who understands that A and B are ethically neutral and probabilistic independent events. We take the next four axioms to be rational. One of these—Monotonicity, which has a similar role as independence in the Von Neumann-Morgenstern system—has been objected to by some serious theoreticians. The remaining three axioms—Equivalence of the Ethically Neutral Events, Intern Operation, and Commutativity—are immediate rational consequences of the concept "ethically neutral."

The following axioms hold for all x, y, z, and w in X:

- *Monotonicity*: Let y and z be in X_1 and $E = A, B$. Then (i) $y \prec z$ if and only if $(x, E, y) \prec (x, E, z)$, and (ii) $y \sim z$ if and only if $(x, E, y) \sim (x, E, z)$.
- *Equivalence of Ethically Neutral Events*: $(x, A, y) \sim (x, B, y) \sim (x, \bar{B}, y) \sim (x, \bar{A}, y)$.
- *Intern*: If $x \prec y$ then $x \prec (x, A, y) \prec y$, $x \prec (x, B, y) \prec y$, $x \prec (x, \bar{B}, y) \prec y$, and $x \prec (x, \bar{A}, y) \prec y$.
- *Idempotent*: $(x, A, x) \sim x$.
- *Commutativity*: $(x, A, y) \sim (y, A, x)$ and $(x, B, y) \sim (y, B, x)$.

To formulate "bisymmetry," gambles of gambles have to be considered. Let A and B be ethically neutral probabilistic independent events. Then the equation,

$$((x, A, y), B, (z, A, w)) = (x, B \cap A; y, B \cap \bar{A}; z, \bar{B} \cap A; w, \bar{B} \cap \bar{A}), \qquad 11.6$$

stands for the following: Left side of Equation 11.6: If B occurs, then the gamble (x, A, y) is played. If then A occurs, x is received; if instead $\bar{A}$ occurs, then y is received. If $\bar{B}$ (instead of B) occurs, then the gamble (z, A, w) is played. If then A occurs, z is received; if instead $\bar{A}$ occurs, then w is received. The right-hand side of Equation 11.6 states exactly this in a different notation, where a term of the form "p,F" stands for receiving pleasure p if event F occurs. Similarly,

$$((x, A, z), B, (y, A, w)) = (x, B \cap A; z, B \cap \bar{A}; y, \bar{B} \cap A; w, \bar{B} \cap \bar{A}). \qquad 11.7$$

Because by probabilistic independence $B \cap A$, $B \cap \bar{A}$, $\bar{B} \cap A$, and $\bar{B} \cap \bar{A}$ should all be given the same weight (i.e., probability $\frac{1}{4}$) in determining the utilities right-hand sides of Equations 11.6 and 11.7, one sees that the right-hand sides describe the same state of affairs, and therefore the left-hand sides describes the same gamble, that is,

- *Bisymmetry*: $((x, A, y), B, (z, A, w)) \sim ((x, A, z), B, (y, A, w))$ holds.

To insure the existence of an appropriate utility function onto the real numbers, the following axiom is needed:

- *Solvability*: If $x \prec y$, then there exist p and q in X_0 such that $x \sim (p, A, y)$ and $y \sim (x, A, q)$.

Define $\oplus$ on X as follows: for all x and y in X and $E = A, \bar{A}, B, \bar{B}$,

$$x \oplus y = (x, E, y).$$

It then follows from Insensitivity Across Ethically Neutral Events that $\oplus$ is an operation on X. It follows from the above assumptions that $\mathfrak{X} = \langle X, \precsim, \oplus \rangle$ is a bisection structure.[14] Thus by Theorem 6 there exists a representation u from an interval scale of representations from $\mathfrak{X}$ onto the reals $\mathbb{R}$ such that for all x and y in X,

$$u(x \oplus y) = \frac{1}{2}[u(x) + u(y)].$$

Appendix 11.4. Cross-Modality Commutativity

Let $\langle X, \leq_1 \rangle$ and $\langle Y, \leq_2 \rangle$ be continua, $X \cap Y = \varnothing$, p and q be > 1, and $w = f_p(x)$ stand for the subject is presented stimulus x from X and w is the stimulus in X that the subject produces in response to "Find the stimulus in Y that is p-times as intense as x." In a similar manner $z = \beta_q(y)$ is defined for stimuli y from Y. Also cross-modal magnitude judgments $z = F_p(x)$ are considered: "For x in X find the z in Y that is p-times intense as x." (Lower case English letters will be used for magnitude production functions on X; lower case Greek letters for magnitude functions on Y, and upper case English letters for cross-modal magnitude functions from X into Y.) Suppose ratio scales representations γ and ψ have been determined, respectively, on X and Y through magnitude functions based on them. Luce et al. (2010) investigated the following question: When do these determine a ratio scale on $X \cup Y$? Their answer is, when

$$\alpha_q[F_p(x)] = \beta_p[F_q(x)]. \tag{11.8}$$

---

[14] This means that $\mathfrak{X}$ satisfies Weakly Ordered Continua, Monotonicity, Commutativity, Bisymmetry, and Solvability with A, B, $\bar{A}$, and $\bar{B}$ replaced by $\oplus$.

Equation 11.8 is called *cross-modal commutativity*. One starts with x in X. Then finds $y = F_p(x)$ in Y that is p-times intense as x; then find z in Y that is q-times as intense as y. Cross-modal commutativity says that if the additional magnitude judgments, "Find $w = F_q(x)$ in Y that is q-times intense as x," followed by "Find v in Y that is p-times intense as w," then $z = v$. It is phrased as starting from X. Another form starts from Y, but is not needed for the following theorem.

Theorem 13 *There exists a ratio scale Δ on $X \cup Y$ such that Δ restricted to X is γ, Δ restricted to Y is ψ, and for each p, the image of F_p under Δ, $\Delta(F_p)$, is interpreted as a ratio.*

The natural interpretation of Theorem 13 is that the subject has a single internal intensity ratio scale Δ for measuring her subjective intensities for stimuli from X and Y. Luce et al. (2010) show for loudness of different tones and Steingrimssion et al. (2012) show for brightness of different colors that Theorem 13 holds experimentally. Note that this theorem *does not require*:

$$f_p, \text{ interpreted as a ratio under } \Delta \text{ [i.e., } \Delta(f_p)) = \gamma(f_p)], \qquad 11.9$$
$$= \alpha_p, \text{ interpreted as a ratio under } \Delta \text{ [i.e., } \Delta(\alpha_p)) = \psi(\alpha_p)],$$
$$= F_p, \text{ interpreted as a ratio under } \Delta \text{ [i.e., } \Delta(f_p))].$$

Let's call Equation 11.9 *cross-modal production coherence*. Luce et al. and Steingrimsson et al. showed that it failed in their experiments. For example, they took an x from X, found a y in Y that was $F_2(x)$ and then found a z that was $\beta_3(y)$. Starting again with x in X, they found an a in X that was $f_2(x)$ and a b in X that was $f_3(a)$. They then asked the subject to find the stimulus c in X that was the same intensity as $z = \alpha_3[F_2(x)]$ in Y. In all cases, $\Delta(z)$ was larger than $\Delta(c)$, contradicting Equation 11.9.

Luce (2004) developed a model that predicted the holding of Theorem 13 and the failure of cross-modal production coherence. His model works as follows: Instead of representing the magnitude production function f_p as a ratio r, where

$$r = \frac{\psi[\phi(y)]}{\psi[\phi(x)]}$$

where ϕ is the physical intensity function, ψ is the psychological intensity function, and $y = f_p(x)$, Luce (2004) represents it as,

$$r = \frac{\psi[\phi(y)] - \psi[\phi(e)]}{\psi[\phi(x)] - \psi[\phi(e)]},$$

where e is a constant—called the *reference point*—that depends on the continuum X and not on x and y. Narens' model is the special case of Luce's where $\psi[\phi(e)] = 0$. Thus, in Luce's modeling, changing continua can change reference points, and this can produce a failure of cross-modality production coherence, as seen in the Luce et al. (2010) and Steingrimsson et al. (2012) experiments. For a complete exposition, see Luce et al. (2010).

It is natural to interpret Theorem 13 and cross-modal production coherence in terms of a ratio scale representation Δ of an internal subjective scale $\mathcal{S}$ on the subject's sensations that arise from stimuli in $X \cup Y$. Stimuli x from X and y from Y are said to be *matched* if and only if $\Delta(x) = \Delta(y)$. It is reasonable to expect if empirically tested for by asking subjects to "Choose the y in Y that matches x in X in subjective intensity," produces such a match. We say that *cross-modal ordinal coherence* holds for Δ when for w and x in X and y and z in Y,

$$w \leq_1 x \text{ if and only if } \Delta(w) \leq_2 \Delta(x),$$

and similarly for y and z in $\langle Y, \leq_2 \rangle$.

It is cross-modal production coherence that is potentially problematic. In the above experiments, it fails. It can fail in different ways, but the analysis of the failure provided next extends to all the ways. To be specific, suppose the failure results from finding x, a, y, and b are such that $f_4(x) = a$ and $g_4(y) = b$, and

$$\Delta(x) = \Delta(y) \text{ and } \Delta(a) \neq \Delta(b).$$

Then for a stimulus z, in computing $\Delta(z)$, the subject does not compute the pure subjective intensity of z, but computes the intensity of z using properties from the dimension that z came from. The subject is not able to abstract the intensity from the stimulus or, put differently, ignore in making her judgment on properties of the stimulus that are irrelevant to the *cardinal* size of the subjective intensity of the stimulus. She, however, still can make coherent *ordinal* intensity judgments (i.e., cross-modal ordinal coherence may hold), and have all the stimuli simultaneously measured on a ratio scale (Theorem 13).

There are many psychophysical studies that show the holding of cross-modal ordinal comparability. The above Luce et al. (2010) and Steingrimsson et al. (2012) studies are the only ones we know of that tests cross-modal production coherence. We conjecture that cross-modal production coherence will fail for different kinds of pleasure. This would cause problems for classical Utilitarianism.

Appendix 11.5. Aggregation of Utilities for a Single Individual

The utility situation under consideration is where a person—call him Adam—has a utility representation U over states of the world. He wants to coordinate with another person—call her Eve—to achieve a perceived joint maximum utility over states x and y when Nature provides him with x and Eve with y. He doesn't know Eve's utility scale V, but he has a cognitive representation of it, which is denoted by U_e. It is measured by Adam in terms of his utility representation U. (Chapter 13 discusses a way U_e might arise.) Thus if $U_e(y) > U(x)$, then Adam perceives y has having more value to Eve than x has for him. Because U_e is measured in terms of U, it undergoes the same set of scale transformations as U; thus if U is properly transformed by T, then U_e is also appropriately transformed by the same transformation T, and vice versa. This provides us with a means to evaluate the meaningfulness of functions that depend on U and U_e.

The following is the main difference between Adam's utility situation and a psychophysical one: In the psychophysical situation, the measurement representation is founded on Adam's perception of his sensations; in Adam's utility case the measurement part involving U_e is founded on the cognitive representation he uses to model Eve's utility judgments. In both situations, there is a single mind viewing the same scale on two different measurement representations. We call this kind of aggregation *intrapersonal*. It should be distinguished from *interpersonal aggregation*, which is the aggregation of two utility functions from different minds. Meaningfulness considerations involving interpersonal aggregations are discussed in Chapter 12.

Let $J_a[U(x), U_e(y)]$ stand for Adam's subjective aggregation of the utility of x, $U(x)$, with his perception of Eve's utility for y, $U_e(y)$. Call J_a *Adam's joint aggregation function*. The scale for J_a could be one that Adam uses, or an outside observer such as a social planner might use, or in the psychophysical case, a scale that the experimenter might use. If Adam is a classical Utilitarian, then he would use the Utilitarian Sum,

$$J_a[U(x), U_e(y)] = U(x) + U_e(y),$$

for measuring his and Eve's joint aggregation. As we will see, this sum itself is not meaningful under interval scalability, but comparisons of it are:

$$U(x) + U_e(y) \leq U(z) + U_e(w).$$

Utilitarianism only needs comparisons of sums of utilities; it wants to improve joint utilities or find a maximal one, and comparisons are all that is needed for this. But under interval scalability it doesn't make sense to say one joint sum is double another, any more than $10°C$ is double $5°C$. To double meaningfully, one needs a ratio scale or an absolute scale.

A theorem will show that if J_a is interval-scale meaningful, then it is greatly restricted—so much so that it is useless for joint utility aggregation. If instead J_a is ratio scale meaningful, then its meaningfulness is also greatly restricted, but less so and in a different manner than the interval-scale case.

The argument for the interval scalable case depends on the following three assumptions:

(i) U and U_e are onto the real numbers.
(ii) $J_a[U(x), U_e(y)]$ is strictly increasing in $U(x)$ and $U_e(y)$.
(iii) J_a and J_e are meaningful under any transformation chosen from their common set of interval-scale transformations.

A little algebraic manipulation, of equation 3.5 of Luce and Narens (1985: 27) to this situation yields the following theorem:

Theorem 14 *All solutions for the aggregating function $J_a[U(p), U_e(q)]$ satisfying assumptions (i)–(iii) above have the following form:*

$$J_a[U(p), U_e(q)] = \frac{1}{2}U(p) + \frac{1}{2}U_e(q) + c|U(p) - U_e(q)|, \qquad 11.10$$

where $0 \leq |c| < \frac{1}{2}$.

Equation 11.10 can be rewritten as,

$$J_a[U(p), U_e(q)] = aU(p) + bU_e(q), \qquad 11.11$$

where $0 < a < 1$ and $0 < b < 1$.[15] This violates Adam's moral imperative that the joint aggregation should not leave both him and Eve worst off than they would be if they did not participate in the joint aggregation; that is, Adam should not engage in a collaborative relationship with Eve if he believes the result of the collaboration will always provide less utility for each of them than both acting separately. While this principle makes moral sense for Adam's utility theory, its equivalent in some psychophysical situations fails empirically.

A less stringent concept of meaningfulness is to require J_a to be only order meaningful instead of meaningful. Then, as discussed earlier,

$$J_a[U(x), U_e(y)] = U(x) + U_e(y)$$

is order meaningful, because for $r > 0$ and s real,

$$r[U(x) + U_e(y)] + s \leq r[U(w) + U_e(z)] + s$$
$$\text{iff } [(rU(x) + s) + (rU_e(y) + s) + s] \leq [(rU(w) + s) + (rU_e(z) + s) + s]$$
$$\text{iff } rU(x) + rU_e y) \leq rU(x) + rU_e(w)$$
$$\text{iff } U(x) + U(y) \leq U(w) + U(z).$$

Theorem 14 shows that interval scalability greatly restricts set of possibilities for meaningful aggregating functions. Ratio scalability, however, provides a weaker form of invariance and consequently a wider variety of meaningful aggregating functions. There are also good theoretical and empirical reasons for assuming ratio scaled utility.[16] However, ratio invariance is still strong enough to severely restrict the form of the aggregation utility function if other general conditions is assumed. The following theorem is from Cohen and Narens (1979: 216), which provides an example of one of these.

Theorem 15 *Suppose J is ratio scale meaningful on the non-negative real numbers and has the power series expansion,*

$$J(w, z) = \sum_{i,j} b_{ij} w^i z^j,$$

---

[15] If $U(p) \geq U_e(q)$ then $0 < a = \frac{1}{2} + c < 1$ because $|c| < \frac{1}{2}$, and $0 < b = \frac{1}{2} - c < 1$ because $|c| < \frac{1}{2}$, and similarly for the case where $U(q) \geq U_e(p)$.
[16] For example, see Luce (2000).

where w and z range over the positive reals, i and j range over the non-negative integers, and J(0, 0) = 0. Then

$$J(w, z) = b_{01}w + b_{10}z.$$

Furthermore, if J is strictly increasing in each variable, then b_{01} and b_{10} are positive.[17]

A special case of Theorem 15 is when

$$J = J_a \text{ and } J_a[U(x), U_e(y)] = U(x) + U_e(y).$$

This provides a natural version of Sum Utilitarianism from Adam's perspective, because it looks like Adam is engaging in a subjective form of Sum Utilitarianism.

Most scholars in economics and philosophy assume utility is measured on an interval scale. But some in these disciplines and many in psychology believe ratio scales are more appropriate. If we assume ratio scalability and restrict Adam's joint utility to the large class of joint utility functions having power series representations, then, by Theorem 15, the only possibilities are functions of the form,

$$J_a[U(x), U_e(y)] = rU(x) + sU_e(y). \qquad 11.12$$

Because J_a is strictly increasing in each variable, r and s are positive. It is natural for Adam to take into account the context in which x and y are realized. For example, if Adam and Eve are on a date, then being with Eve may enhance the joy x brings to Adam thus increasing $U(x)$ from what

---

[17] **Proof**. From $J(0, 0) = 0$ it follows that $b_{00} = 0$. Let r be a positive real. Then, because J is meaningful,

$$rJ(w, z) = J(rw, rz),$$

and thus

$$rJ(w, z) - J(rw, rz) = 0$$

for all w and z. In terms of the power series representation, this yields,

$$r\sum_{i,j} b_{ij}w^i z^j - \sum_{ij} b_{i,j}(rw)^i (rz)^j = \sum_{i,j} b_{i,j}w^i z^j (r - r^i r^j) = 0.$$

By assumption $b_{00} = 0$. If either $i > 1$ or $j > 1$, then $r - r^i r^j \neq 0$, and thus $b_{ij} = 0$. Thus non-zero terms can only occur when $i = 0$ and $j = 1$ or when $i = 1$ and $j = 0$. In such a case all other terms are 0. Thus for all positive w and z,

$$J(w, z) = b_{01}w + b_{10}z.$$

he would have experienced separately. One might be tempted to choose a $r > 1$ in Equation 11.12 to capture this enhancement. But it won't work. It says that all elements of X are enhanced by the same proportion r, and this is unreasonable. More reasonable is for Adam to distinguish x experienced alone, call it "x no date" or "x_{nd}" for short, from x experienced on a date with Eve, "x_d," and expand X to X' include these and other context influenced elements, and similarly for U_e. Then assume that we started with the expanded domain instead of X. Equation 11.12 then becomes,

$$J_a[U(x), U_e(y)] = U(x) + U_e(y) = J_a[U_e(y), U(x)]. \qquad 11.13$$

The resulting commutativity of J_a expressed in Equation 11.13 can be viewed as a moral rule. Note that the assumptions behind it did not directly invoke aggregation additivity. It instead followed from ratio scalability, meaningfulness, strict monotonicity in each variable, and having a power series for $J_a[U(x), U_e(y)]$ with $J(0, 0) = 0$—none of which individually suggest commutativity.

PART III

INTERPERSONAL COMPARISONS AND CONVENTION

12

Product Utilitarianism and an Old-New Way to Measure Utility

Now suppose happiness to consist in doing or choosing the greater, and in not doing or in avoiding the less, what would be the saving principle of human life? Would not the art of measuring be the saving principle; or would the power of appearance? Is not the latter that deceiving art which makes us wander up and down and take the things at one time of which we repent at another, both in our actions and in our choice of things great and small?

(Socrates in *Protagoras*)

To precise the ideas, let there be granted to the science of pleasure what is granted to the science of energy; to imagine an ideally perfect instrument, a psychophysical machine, continually registering the height of pleasure experienced by an individual, exactly according to the verdict of consciousness, or rather diverging therefrom according to a law of errors. From moment to moment the hedonimeter varies; the delicate index now flickering with the flutter of the passions, now steadied by intellectual activity, low sunk whole hours in the neighbourhood of zero, or momentarily springing up towards infinity. The continually indicated height is registered by photographic or other frictionless apparatus upon a uniformly moving vertical plane. Then the quantity of happiness between two epochs is represented by the area contained between the zero-line, perpendiculars thereto at the points corresponding to the epochs, and the curve traced by the index.

(Edgeworth in *Mathematical Psychics*)

The Pursuit of Happiness: Philosophical and Psychological Foundations of Utility. Louis Narens and Brian Skyrms, Oxford University Press (2020). © Louis Narens and Brian Skyrms.
DOI: 10.1093/oso/9780198856450.001.0001

12.1 Introduction

Pleasure can be measured, and measurement of pleasure can be used as a tool for improving our lives. This is an old idea that Edgeworth recast in terms of integral calculus. For him, pleasure does not come in particles, to be counted as did Bentham, but rather as a continuous quantity. The total pleasure of an episode is the integral of pleasure intensity over time. This idea can be resurrected in modern form, not from neurobiology, but rather from preferences. The resulting theory goes some way towards delivering a meaningful form of Utilitarianism. Meaningful aggregation of utilities, which eludes us on the Von Neumann-Morgenstern approach is now possible, with some twists and turns and some restrictions.

We revisit Edgeworth's hedonimeter by connecting and generalizing two ideas.[1] The first is that there is a representation theorem possible for hedonic value similar to, but also importantly different from, the one provided by Von Neumann and Morgenstern to measure decision-based utility. The idea is to use objective duration, in place of objective chance, to measure hedonic value. This line of thought is developed in Kahneman Wakker et al.'s (1997) "Back to Bentham." We pursue a somewhat different development of the same basic idea. These representations for hedonic value deliver a stronger kind of scale than Von Neumann-Morgenstern utility, because there is a natural zero point, whereas in Von Neumann-Morgenstern the choice of zero point is arbitrary.[2] Hedonic utility is measured on a ratio scale. On the Von Neumann-Morgenstern approach, utility is measured on a weaker interval scale.

The second idea is that measurement on a ratio scale allows a kind of meaningful aggregation of utilities over a group. For aggregation to be meaningful it must give results that are invariant over arbitrary choices of parameters of the measurement scales for individuals comprising the group. The natural zero of the hedonic value scale makes a kind of Utilitarian aggregation of pleasures meaningful that is not meaningful on an interval scale. This is aggregation by product of individual utilities.[3] More precisely, the ordering of aggregate pleasure by product is invariant over choice of unit. *We emphasize that we now have meaningful aggregation without postulating*

---

[1] Ideas on this chapter come from Skyrms and Narens (2019).

[2] One way in which we differ from Kahnemann et al., is the way we identify a natural zero point, They postulate a zero intensity for pleasure. We find a natural zero in a null episode.

[3] Or equivalently by sum of the logarithms of individual utilities.

interpersonal comparisons of utilities. Since this is aggregation by product rather than sum, it is not quite classical Utilitarianism, but it is closely related.

Aggregation of pleasures (of positive hedonic values) by product has Prioritarian consequences. That is to say that under Product Utilitarianism, to increase aggregate utility it is especially important to help those worse off. It has been independently proposed for this reason. Adler (2011) contains an extensive discussion. The idea is so natural, it has been invented a number of times in different contexts. In 1950 John Nash proposed and axiomatically justified his bargaining solution, which finds a solution to his bargaining problems by choosing the point that maximizes the product of utilities. The disagreement point, where no bargain is struck, serves as a zero.[4] This is generalized to the Nash Social Welfare Function by Kaneko and Nakamura in 1979.[5] To get their zero, they postulate "one of the worst states for all individuals that we can imagine."[6] It was recently rediscovered as in theoretical computer science as a fair way to allocate network resources.[7] In these contexts, allocation of zero quantities of physical resources gives the natural zero point. We see a lot of different kinds of "zeros" here. But from the Utilitarian standpoint we have been exploring so far, the zero in the utility scale cannot be simply postulated at will. We will bear this in mind in what follows.

When all individuals have negative hedonic values (net pain) meaningful aggregation is still possible, but Priotarianism is lost (and indeed reversed.) When some individuals have positive hedonic values and others negative, all sensible aggregation seems impossible. Restricting ourselves to the positive case, aggregation of pleasures becomes complicated when hedonic value is mixed with uncertainty. Meaningful aggregation is still possible, but can be done in two different ways, and they are not equivalent.

The representation of hedonic value saves some parts of classical Utilitarianism as meaningful, but not others. It should be of interest to proponents of Utilitarianism, as well as opponents, to see what survives as meaningful and what is meaningless. For instance Parfit's "lives barely worth living" assumes a non-arbitrary zero point. Nozick's (1974) "Utility Monster" assumes a non-arbitrary unit. The latter assumption is meaningless on the kind of hedonic utility developed here. Both are meaningless on Von Neumann-Morgenstern

---

[4] Nash (1950).
[5] Kaneko and Nakamura (1979).
[6] p. 423.
[7] Vazirani, V. (2007): ch. 5.

utility measurement. But here we do have a non-arbitrary zero point. Does Parfit's point survive? We will return to this question later in the chapter.

12.2 Episodes

> let us begin with saying: Pleasure is comprised under two dimensions, Intensity and Duration.
>
> (Bentham in Halévy 1995 [1901]: vol. 1, appendix II, p. 302)

For Bentham and Edgeworth the primary bearers of utility for an individual are *episodes*. They are characterized by the times they begin and end, their intensity and duration of pleasure.[8] Duration is the interval of time between their beginning and end. Intensity need not be constant, it is some function over time. Leaving pain to the side for the moment, for Bentham the utility of an episode is gotten by "summing up" the constituent pleasure intensities. In Edgeworth, utility of an episode becomes the integral of pleasure intensity with respect to time, evaluated from the beginning to the end of the episode.[9]

We immediately notice a property of this scheme that may seem counterintuitive; order does not matter: *If episode 2 comes from episode 1 by permuting two sub-episodes of positive duration, then it is a matter of indifference between episode 1 and episode 2.* This may appear to fly in the face of the commonplace that the order of experiences makes a difference in judged overall pleasure. The Benthamite would reply that this confuses order of the experiences that engender pleasure with the order of pleasure intensity. You may like an appetizer before entrée before main before dessert better than other permutations of the courses, but this just shows that permutations of courses do more than permute sub-intervals of pleasure intensity: They change the intensities of pleasure within those sub-intervals.

The second of Bentham's "sovereign masters" is pain. Pains are compared just as pleasures are:

> If of two pains a man would as lief escape one as the other, such two pains must be reputed equal.
>
> (Bentham in Halévy 1995 [1901]: vol. 1, appendix II, p. 302)

---

[8] In this section, we take time to be objective. Of course, if we take it as subjective rather than objective—as Bentham did—the situation becomes more complicated.

[9] The idea is clear in Edgeworth's (1879) *Mind* article and in Edgeworth's (1888 [1881]) appendix III of *Mathematical Psychics*.

In a purely painful episode, the total pain would be the integral of pain intensity over time.

We may have episodes that combine both pleasure and pain. How are they to be treated? First we have to ask what kinds of combinations are possible. We may have episodes that are pleasurable for a stretch of time and painful for a stretch. Can we have also episodes that are both pleasurable to some extent and painful to some extent at the same time? How do pleasure and pain interact in determining the utility of an episode? Is it possible that someone might prefer a pleasure with a small amount of pain to pure pleasure?

Bentham insists that the interaction of pleasure and pain is purely additive. Thus,

> If of two sensations, a pain and a pleasure, a man would as lief enjoy the pleasure and suffer the pain, as not enjoy the first and not suffer the latter, such pleasure and pain must be reputed equal.
>
> (Bentham in Halévy 1995 [1901]: vol. 1, appendix II, p. 302)

and

> Sum up all the values of all the pleasures on the one side, and those of all the pains on the other. The balance, if it be on the side of pleasure, will give the good tendency of the act upon the whole, with respect to the interests of that individual person; if on the side of pain, the bad tendency of it upon the whole.[10]

That is to say that pleasure and pain are put on the same scale, with pleasure intensities being positive values and pain intensities being negative values. The hedonic value of an episode is the integral of this hedonic value function over time, and may itself be positive, negative or zero. There is a modern representation theorem for just this conception of hedonic value.

12.3 Representation of Hedonic Value

We discuss this in two stages. In the first we choose some fixed time period and draw out the parallel with the Von Neumann-Morgenstern

---

[10] Bentham(1789): ch. IV, section V. The setting here is different. Bentham is thinking of JNDs. But the principle is clear.

representation. Then we proceed to episodes of variable duration. To start, recall Von Neumann-Morgenstern from Section 7.1. There is a set of prospects. A subject is assumed to have preferences over chance distributions over prospects. (These are sometimes called "lotteries" to provide a vivid image of the objective chances, but no actual lottery procedure is implied.) Under the assumption that preferences are a total ordering of these "lotteries" that satisfies independence and continuity conditions,[11] it is shown that a utility exists such that preference over lotteries goes by their expected utilities. The expected utilities for two lotteries are equal just in case the subject is indifferent between them. The expected utility of one is higher than another just in case the subject prefers it to the other. The utilities are unique up to arbitrary choice of zero and unit. If we add or subtract a constant to all utilities we get the same preferences, and if we multiply all utilities by a positive constant, we get the same preferences. *The position of the zero point, and the size of a unit on the scale do not derive any empirical meaning from the preference ordering.* This is an interval scale.

Compare hedonic episodes over a fixed time period, one hour or one day or one year. Hedonic intensities are analogous to prospects. Episodes are analogous to lotteries over prospects. An episode with with $\frac{2}{3}$ of the time at intensity A and $\frac{1}{3}$ of the time at intensity B is like a lottery with chance $\frac{2}{3}$ of getting A and chance $\frac{1}{3}$ of getting B. With some not inconsiderable idealization of the psychology, the Von Neumann-Morgenstern representation (or rather a modern generalization, see Kreps 1988: ch 5) can be applied.[12] There is an integral representation of hedonic value of episodes. But at this point, we have only an interval scale. Choice of zero and unit are still arbitrary.

Now consider the extension to measurements of hedonic values of intervals of arbitrary duration. Two non-overlapping episodes can be concatenated to make a composite episode. Order does not matter. Measurement at some fixed intensity proceeds just like measurement of length. Hedonic value of episodes adds. There is an integral representation of hedonic value of episodes along these lines in Kahneman et al. (1997) and Sarin and Wakker (1997). Notice that no matter what the intensities, the null episode of zero duration must have zero hedonic value. We now have a natural non-arbitrary zero point for hedonic value of episodes. This gives a natural zero

---

[11] Together with a few other technical conditions.

[12] We are indebted to a reader for pointing out that continuity, completeness of the order, and the Archimedean property are all psychologically questionable. These idealizations are far from Bentham.

for intensities, the intensity such that a positive duration of it is an episode of the same hedonic value as the null episode. Hedonic values are now measured on a scale with arbitrary unit, but a meaningful zero. This zero can be taken as marking the Utilitarians' divide between pleasure and pain.

12.4 Aggregation of Pleasures

Consider a stretch of time, where the members of a group of finite size remain constant. Assume that the net hedonic value of the episode for each member of the group is positive. How can utility of the group be meaningfully quantified? Bentham thought that we should take the sum of the hedonic values of the individuals. On the foregoing account it cannot be as a sum, because individual utilities are only measured up to an arbitrary unit. Multiply Peter's units by one constant and Paul's by another and, provided their interests conflict, you may reverse the pair's group preferences. Bear in mind that on the account of measurement given in the last section, the units do not correspond to anything in reality. Thus the ordering of Peter's and Paul's sum is not meaningful.

The foregoing account, unlike that of Von Neumann-Morgenstern, has a distinguished zero, and measures each individual's utilities on a ratio scale. Choice of unit is arbitrary, but choice of zero is not. We can now measure aggregate utility for the group by the product of individual utilities rather than the sum. Then multiplying Peter's and Paul's utilities by a positive real number has the property that it preserves the numerical ordering of the aggregates of individual episodes no matter which representation from individuals' ratio scales are used. For example, Suppose u is Peter's utility function and v is Paul's, and for pleasures A and B, suppose $u(A)v(A) \leq u(B)V(B)$, $u(A)$, $v(B)$ positive. Multiply Peter's utilities by one positive constant c, and Paul's by another, d, and we see that the scale changes cancel out.[13] The product is meaningful for aggregate orderings. We call such product aggregation the *Utilitarian Product*.

Consider the following example comparing the Product and Sum Utility aggregations. Suppose that Peter has utility 5 for A and 4 for B, and Paul

---

[13] It turns out given standard continuity and monotonicity conditions for aggregation, then any other aggregation that *meaningfully* preserved orderings yields the same ordering as taking the product of utilities. This result holds for any number ≥ 2 of individual utility functions as long as the individual utilities are all positive. See Aczél and Roberts (1989) for details and proof.

has utility 2 for A and 3 for B. Peter prefers A; Paul prefers B. The group, going by product, prefers B (4×3) to A (5×2), so the group preference goes with Paul. Now we change Peter's scale by multiplication by 100. Peter now values A at 500 and B at 400. The group, going by product, has the same preferences, preferring B ($100 \times 4 \times 3$) to A ($100 \times 5 \times 2$). The scale change cancels out. Observe that if we had used the sum, rather than the product, the scale change would have changed the group preference to favor Peter, 502 to 403. The sum is not meaningful for aggregate ordering; the product is.

Aggregation by product is not only meaningful for comparisons, but it has properties of independent interest. It has been suggested by Adler[14] and others for its Prioritarian flavor, as is evident in the following examples.

Suppose that a windfall has been found and the feasible social options under consideration all give each member of the group positive utility. Then we can use the product to aggregate. For instance, new trees appear in the garden of Eden, and there is new fruit to distribute. Adam and Eve can enjoy them over the time period in question. Distribution (A) gives Adam utility 1 on one version of his ratio scale, and Eve 20 on one version of hers, while distribution (B) gives Adam 5 and Eve 5. We resist the urge to look at the sum which is meaningless; we look at the product. Then (B), with a product of 25 is socially preferable to (A) with a product of 10. If we multiply Adam's utilities by one positive constant and Eve's by another, (B) is still preferable to (A). We must note that by choosing the constants, we could make (A) look more egalitarian than (B) because "egalitarian" doesn't really mean anything in this framework. Suppose that we multiply Adam's utiles by 20, and leave Eve's alone. Then, in this representation, (A) looks egalitarian, but Adam does so well in (B) that the aggregate good favors (B).

If we know that Adam's utility (on some version of his ratio scale) is a function of the quantity of some real or monetary good possessed, and likewise for Eve, then we can do more. Consider the case of dividing \$100 between Adam and Eve, with the proviso that each must get at least \$1. On some choice of units for their ratio scales, Adam's utility function is $u(\$x) = x$ and Eve's is $v(\$x) = \sqrt{x}$. In this case, if the Utilitarian Sum were meaningful, the only Utilitarian Sum solution (the distribution that maximizes the sum of their utilities) would be \$99 to Adam and \$1 to Eve. The Utilitarian product solution is $\frac{2}{3}$\$100 to Adam and $\frac{1}{3}$\$100 to Eve.[15]

---

[14] Adler (2011). Adler uses the Von Neumann-Morgenstern representation, and postulates a zero on ethical grounds. His account is thus quite different in both motivation and character from the one examined here.

[15] For more that can be done with special utility functions, see Appendix 12.1.

We have a way of measuring hedonic value that, so far, allows meaningful aggregation in an interesting way. But we have not yet considered pain.

12.5 Aggregation of Pain

Suppose a disaster is at hand and the members of the group will undergo episodes that give each member net pain. To evaluate these scenarios we need to aggregate negative hedonic values. Obviously we cannot simply take the product, with the sign of the aggregate flipping back and forth as each additional member is factored in. But meaningful aggregation is still possible. We take the negative of the product of the absolute values of the pains. Thus, if Adam and Eve have hedonic values −2 and −3, the aggregate is −6. Pain can be aggregated in a perfectly meaningful way.

But we must notice that the Prioritarian flavor of product aggregation that has been remarked on in the aggregation of pleasures is now reversed. Adam and Eve face two alternative scenarios which affect how they will share the pain. Scenario (A) gives Adam utility −1 on one version of his ratio scale, and Eve −20 on one version of hers, while distribution (B) gives Adam −5 and Eve −5. We again resist the urge to look at the sum which is meaningless for comparisons. We aggregate as above. Then (A), with aggregate pain of −20 is socially preferable to (B) with aggregate pain of −25.

Those who have advocated product aggregation on Prioritarian grounds without taking pains into account should have food for thought.

12.6 Aggregation of Mixed Pleasure and Pain

Suppose that we wish to compare hedonic values for episodes in which some members of the group have net pleasure and others have net pain. We can meaningfully compare the pleasures and the pains separately, as shown in the foregoing. There is an aggregate group pleasure and an aggregate group pain. But how are they to be combined to get a group hedonic value?

We cannot simply subtract the group pain from the group pleasure to get group hedonic value. This will not allow meaningful comparisons. Multiplying individual's hedonic values by arbitrary positive constants could then reverse group hedonic ordering. On our way of measuring individual pleasures and pains, this additive conception of group hedonic value is quite without meaning.

It is evident that the quotient, the value of group pleasure over the absolute value to group pain, will not do either. A tiny amount of group pain would blow up the quotient, giving the result that a state where someone would be slightly unhappy would be better than one the same except that that person was slightly happy. And since pain is measured on a ratio scale, there is no meaningful distinction between aggregate pain less that 1 and aggregate pain greater than 1. And what about zero pain?

We could try absolute value of group pleasure over 1 plus absolute value of group pain. This would at least have the property that zero pain gives a group hedonic value equal to total pleasure. But this does not yield meaningful comparisons. Suppose that in scenario *A*, Eve gets pleasure of magnitude 2 and Adam pain of magnitude 1 and in scenario *B* Eve gets pleasure of magnitude 1 and Adam is has neither pleasure nor pain. Adam is at 0. Then Eve prefers *A* and Adam prefers *B*, and the proposed aggregation rule counts them as, on balance, equal. But if we multiply Adam's units by 10 the aggregation rule favors *B* and, if we multiply them by .1, it favors *A*.

At this point we see no obvious way to combine group pleasure and pain so that such combinations can be meaningfully compared. In what follows we confine the discussion to positive hedonic values.

12.7 Parfit's Counterexamples

The foregoing discussion deals with a fixed population. If the alternative scenarios being evaluated involve different populations, then things are different. In that context, Parfit (1984) raised a difficulty for Utilitarianism thus:

> For any possible population of at least ten billion people, all with a very high quality of life, there must be some much larger imaginable population whose existence, if other things are equal, would be better even though its members have lives that are barely worth living.

> (p. 388)

Parfit's "lives barely worth living" presumably assumes a non-arbitrary zero, dividing lives that are worth living from those that are not. According to Von Neumann-Morgenstern utility there is no such zero; all the lives in question could just as well be represented as having negative values; Parfit's argument is meaningless for interval-scale utility. For this reason, modern decision theorists do not think much of Parfit's argument.

But here we do have a non-arbitrary zero point, and all the values assumed in the argument are positive. We have a way of meaningfully aggregating positive hedonic values. So one might well wonder whether we have not made some version of Parfit's argument, taking lives as hedonic episodes, meaningful.

The answer is negative. A different kind of comparison is being made, and we must be careful with meaningfulness in the context where we are adding or subtracting members of the group. Adding a life with utility 2 doubles the product; adding a life with utility .5 cuts it in half. But utility of 1 is not meaningful when utilities are measured on a ratio scale. It is not meaningful to ask whether adding a life with positive utility increases or decreases the aggregate.

Parfit (1984) has another argument, in the same framework, against those who would compare populations using the arithmetic average. A population with a few extremely happy people has an average utility higher than one which, in addition, has many people who are almost, but not quite, as happy.

> Suppose that Adam and Eve lived these wonderful lives. On the Average Principle it would be worse if, *not instead but in addition*, the billion billion other people lived. [Note: Specified earlier as having a quality of life almost as high.] This would be worse because it would lower the average quality of life.
>
> (p. 420)

On our measurement of pleasures for a fixed population comparisons with the arithmetic averages are not meaningful, but the geometric mean[16] are. Consider Perfit's second argument using the geometric mean. On one representation, Adam has utility 101. We could add Eve who, on one representation, would have utility 100. This would decrease the geometric mean so, by Parfit's second argument, it would argue for leaving Adam alone. But Eve's utilities could just as well be rescaled to 1,000, which would increase the geometric mean. Or to 101, which would leave it unchanged. Likewise for all those other people. In our measurement setting, both of Parfit's arguments

---

[16] The arithmetic mean of n values is gotten by adding them together and dividing them by n. The geometric mean is gotten by multiplying them together and taking the nth root. It produces the same ordering on the fixed population's utilities as the product.

fail to be meaningful.[17] It is not the size of a particular product or geometric mean that is meaningful, but their comparison for the *same* population.

An anonymous reader made the interesting suggestion that a version of Parfit's first argument applies at the individual level. A long life with very small intensity of pleasure throughout would have greater hedonic value as an episode than a short life with high intensity of pleasure. This certainly follows from the integral representation. We do not think that Bentham would disagree. In fact, one of his arguments for the contemplative pleasures was that they could be sustained over a long time.

12.8 Chance

In his (1822) *Codification Proposal*, and elsewhere, Bentham called attention to the role of chance in evaluating prospects for future episodes. This is where Bentham comes in contact with Von Neumann and Morgenstern. We consider only the most tractable case of positive hedonic values. There are still complications, but not insuperable difficulties.

Suppose that a Utilitarian's choices do not determine a forthcoming episode, but rather a gamble over possible episodes. How should she value such gambles? Bentham says to take the expectation. This is not uncontroversial, but we pursue Bentham's suggestion here. Suppose an individual's utilities are extended to probability distributions over possible episodes in this way.

A social planner may also face choices of gambles over episodes. How should the Utilitarian planner value such gambles? Two possible approaches present themselves for positive utilities. Because we are assuming ratio scaled utilities, footnote 13 applies, and thus we must use product aggregation or a related aggregation principle that orders aggregations in the same manner as the Utilitarian product in order to preserve meaningfulness. We will use the product rule.

---

[17] A reader suggests that we may be somewhat unfair to Parfit, since he has a different conception of utility from what we discuss. We would insist, however, that questions of measurement and meaningfulness are still relevant for any conception of utility. In 2012: 203, Parfit explicitly prescinds from such questions, and simply postulates numerical values. We have shown that such questions cannot simply be ignored. See also the discussion of Parfit in Otsuka (2015).

(1) First, aggregate utilities of episodes by product; second, planner takes expectations to get utilities of lotteries.

(2) First, individuals take expectations to get utilities of lotteries; second, planner aggregates utilities of lotteries by product.

These two approaches do not give the same result.

We illustrate with a simple example:

- Adam has Utilities 1, 3, 5 for prospects A, B, C respectively.
- Eve has Utilities 5, 3, 1 from prospects A, B, C respectively.
- There is also a lottery $<\frac{1}{2}A, \frac{1}{2}C>$, giving A or C, each with probability $\frac{1}{2}$.

(1) first aggregates prospects by product, giving 5, 9, 5 to A, B, C. Then extends to lotteries by expectation, giving:

$$\begin{array}{|cccc|} A & B & C & <\frac{1}{2}A, \frac{1}{2}C> \\ 5 & 9 & 5 & 5 \end{array}$$

(2) first has each individual extend to lotteries by expectation:

$$\begin{array}{|l|cccc|} & A & B & C & <\frac{1}{2}A, \frac{1}{2}C> \\ \text{Adam} & 1 & 3 & 5 & 3 \\ \text{Eve} & 5 & 3 & 1 & 3 \end{array}$$

Then aggregates by product:

$$\begin{array}{|cccc|} A & B & C & <\frac{1}{2}A, \frac{1}{2}C> \\ 5 & 9 & 5 & 9 \end{array}$$

With each of the alternatives we lose a property of the social planner's Utilitarian evaluation of gambles that we might wish to retain:

- With alternative (2), the social planner is incoherent. Both A and C have social utility 5, but a 50/50 gamble between them has utility 9 by the product rule. This violates the Von Neumann-Morgenstern independence axiom.[18]

---

[18] Most of those who have questioned the independence axiom would not welcome a deviation in this direction. The social planner here is not risk averse but risk seeking.

- With alternative (1), the social planner flouts consensus. Each individual is indifferent between preferring B to the lottery $< 1/2A, 1/2C >$. But the social planner strictly prefers B to the lottery. This violates a weak form of the Pareto principle.

Given the preceding, there are two, mutually exclusive, versions of Product Utilitarianism. The choice between alternatives (1) and (2) is a choice between group rationality and respect for group consensus. An advocate of alternative (2) might argue that coherence is not all that important. A proponent of alternative (1) might maintain that the *prima facie* plausibility of the Pareto Principle does not hold up under examination. In somewhat different contexts, both sorts of arguments have generated an extensive literature.

Suppose one is not willing to give up either coherence or Pareto. And suppose one follows Bentham in extending utility to gambles by taking the expectation. Harsanyi's theorem (1955) shows that one must be some version of a Sum Utilitarian. In this case one would have to wrestle with the meaningfulness issue that Product Utilitarianism solves.

Appendix 12.1. Primary Goods and Product Utilitarianism

Egalitarianism and Utilitarianism are commonly seen as competing approaches to social philosophy. For instance, John Harsanyi is a kind of modern Utilitarian and John Rawls is a kind of modern Egalitarian. One should, however, not lose sight of the fact that Harsanyi and Rawls are talking about different things. Harsanyi is talking about maximizing aggregate Utility, and Rawls is talking about equal distribution of Primary Goods— which are means to produce Utility. Rawls emphasizes that quantities of primary goods are objectively measurable, and that he thus avoids any necessity for interpersonal comparisons of utility. This raises the question of the relation between the two. Something interesting can be said.

Suppose we confine ourselves to goods that can be traded, are measured on a ratio scale, and are divisible. A distribution of bundles of goods among members of society is *envy-free* if no member of society would prefer another member's bundle to her own.[19] An envy-free distribution can evidently be

---

[19] Foley (1967).

accomplished by each member of society having an equal portion of each good. Each has the same bundle. This allocation of goods may well not be Pareto optimal because people are different. Adam and Eve get equal quantities of gin and equal quantities of vermouth, but Eve likes her Martinis very dry and Adam doesn't. Then there would be good reason for Adam and Eve to trade, until they come to an equilibrium. At equilibrium, they are still envy-free because they only trade when a trade is Pareto improving. And at equilibrium they are at a Pareto optimal state, because if not they would continue to trade. What we have just described is called *competitive equilibrium from equal incomes*.[20] Remember that Pareto optimality means that at equilibrium, they choose a distribution that some version of Sum Utilitarianism would choose on some version of interpersonal comparisons. In this sense, Rawlsian egalitarian endowment of primary goods is compatible with Utilitarianism.

Under the conditions described, for a special class of utility functions, there is also a connection with Product Utilitarianism. Suppose x and y are quantities of two primary goods, and getting none of each gives zero utility. Suppose the utility functions of members of society are *homogeneous*, in the following sense. The utility, $U(x, y)$, given by a bundle x of the first good and y of the second good obeys $U(ax, ay) = aU(x, y)$ for any positive a. Then competitive equilibrium from equal incomes maximizes the Nash Product. Remarkably, equal endowment of primary goods here leads to a distribution that is envy-free, Pareto optimal, and that recommended by Product Utilitarianism. The result holds for any number of divisible primary goods.[21]

Many of the utility functions studied by economists are homogeneous. But the power law utility functions motivated by psychophysics are not. Many of utility functions' interest in computer science, relevant to distribution of computing power or network bandwidth, however, are. This has led to the resurgence of interest in computer science in issues previously discussed by philosophers and economists.[22] Current research focuses on "lumpy" goods, which are not arbitrarily divisible. There the picture is not so pretty. But market mechanisms starting with equal endowments can still approximate product Utilitarian distributions.[23]

---

[20] Varian (1974).
[21] Shafer and Sonnenschein (1982): Theorem 3, p. 636).
[22] For examples and discussion, see Moulin (2003: ch. 7).
[23] Caragiannis et al. (2016).

13

Dynamics of Convention

Sweet exists by convention, bitter by convention, colour by convention; atoms and Void exist in reality.

(Democritus)

13.1 Interpersonal Comparisons by Convention

We have seen just how far modern measurement theory, psychology, and neurobiology can get us in attaching a definite meaning to Utilitarianism. We have perhaps gotten further than many might expect with the Product Utilitarianism of Chapter 12. It at least delivers a coherent view in the case of positive utilities, even if that view is not exactly what classical Utilitarians had in mind. The more orthodox theory of utility measurement in the manner of von Neumann and Morgenstern, does less. It really adds nothing to what one had on the purely ordinal view of utility; the only remnant of Utilitarian moral theory that remains meaningful is Pareto dominance.

There is an alternative view, however, that we have not yet explored.[1] We can, indeed, make interpersonal comparisons of utility of this view, but these comparisons are not findings of fact. Rather they are based on convention. Meanings of words are conventional. Proper syntax is conventional. Social norms are conventional. Might not interpersonal comparisons also be conventional, or at least have an element of convention?

The idea had been floated in the literature. Lionel Robbins, a strict Ordinalist regarding utility measurement, suggested it already in 1938 in a note on interpersonal comparisons.[2] Robbins confesses that he has always been a "provisional Utilitarian," who thinks that Utilitarianism is a best first try at group moral judgments. But the interpersonal comparisons behind the Utilitarian Sum are not based on scientifically ascertainable facts, but

---

[1] Ideas in this chapter come from Narens and Skyrms (2018).
[2] Robbins (1938).

The Pursuit of Happiness: Philosophical and Psychological Foundations of Utility. Louis Narens and Brian Skyrms, Oxford University Press (2020). © Louis Narens and Brian Skyrms.
DOI: 10.1093/oso/9780198856450.001.0001

rather are moral judgments. Social conventions might lead to one kind of interpersonal comparison in one society and another in a different one.

John Harsanyi in 1955[3] agrees: "Professor Robbins is clearly right when he maintains that propositions which purport to be inter personal comparisons of utility often contain a purely conventional element based on ethical or political value judgments." But he then argues that when these conventional elements are put aside, there remains an underlying objective psychological basis for comparison. We have found such a basis remarkably difficult to pin down.

Louis Narens and R. Duncan Luce make the suggestion in a stronger form in a 1983 paper: "How we may have been misled into believing in the interpersonal comparability of utility."[4] Narens and Luce suggest that interpersonal comparisons may be purely conventional, while people believe that they are objective. The conventions are not necessarily moral judgments. People just believe that there is a truth of the matter, which there isn't, and blunder around until they fall into a convention, which they believe is the truth. Multiple conventions are possible, and none is truer than another. Ken Binmore, in his theory of the Social Contract, also has a conventional view of interpersonal comparisons. The view presented in this chapter will have much in common with Binmore.

We see that there are different versions of the view that interpersonal comparisons are conventions. What would such conventions look like, and how might social groups arrive at them?

13.2 Convention

What is a convention? Democritus' definition is unavailable and, in any case, might not be quite what we need. The best answer for our purposes was given by David Hume:

> And this may properly enough be called a convention or agreement betwixt us, though without the interposition of a promise; since the actions of each of us have a reference to those of the other, and are performed upon the supposition, that something is to be performed on the other part. Two men,

---

[3] Harsanyi (1955).
[4] Narens and Luce (1983).

who pull the oars of a boat, do it by an agreement or convention, though they have never given promises to each other.[5]

All modern treatments are developments of Hume's idea.

Two centuries later, after Von Neumann and Morgenstern had developed the theory of games, the philosopher David Lewis used game theory to give a modern formulation of Hume's theory of convention.[6] Lewis' main concern was the conventionality of linguistic meaning, and the claim that logical truths are true by conventions of meaning. But he takes broad notice of the sweep of conventions in social interaction. Lewis' basic idea is that the relevant social interaction is to be modeled as a coordination game, and that a convention is a kind of strict Nash equilibrium of this game. Anyone who unilaterally deviates from such an equilibrium suffers from doing so. Conventions thus acquire a self-enforcing character, so long as the individuals involved are cognizant of what is going on.

Lewis' account has subsequently been refined and generalized, but the basic ideas we have cited remain in subsequent accounts. The self-enforcing property extends from a Nash equilibrium to a correlated equilibrium, where individuals correlate their actions using an external random signal. And using this leads to a correlated convention as proposed by Peter Vanderschraaf.[7] Equilibrium can be understood as a dynamic equilibrium of some adaptive adjustment process, which leads to the transposition of these ideas to evolutionary game theory, as seen in Sugden,[8] Binmore,[9] and Skyrms.[10] The evolutionary turn is already expressed informally in Hume:

Nor is the rule concerning the stability of possession the less derived from human conventions, that it arises gradually, and acquires force by a slow progression, and by our repeated experience of the inconveniences of transgressing it.

We are led to ask not only what a convention of interpersonal comparisons of utility might look like, but also by what adaptive process such a convention might arise.

[5] Hume (1738).
[6] Lewis (1969).
[7] Vanderschraaf (1995).
[8] Sugden (2004 [1986]).
[9] Binmore, K. (1987 a,b, 2008).
[10] Skyrms (1996, 2003, 2010).

13.3   Interpersonal Comparisons in the Garden of Eden

Adam and Eve make interpersonal utility comparisons all the time in the garden of Eden.[11],[12] Adam volunteers to wash the dishes even though Eve would do so otherwise, because he judges that the difference for him is smaller than the difference for Eve, who really hates doing it. He may just do it for Eve's sake. Or he may anticipate a future *quid pro quo*. We focus here on such comparison of differences. How do they do it?

We paint an idealized picture of Adam's and Eve's individual utilities— this is, after all the Garden of Eden—in order to frame our problem. There is a set of outcomes that Adam and Eve both care about. Each has coherent preferences over probabilities over outcomes in the standard way. (At this point we assume egoistic preferences. That is to say they are just about dish washing, and do not yet incorporate the other-regarding elements.) This gives them each orthodox Von Neumann-Morgenstern utilities such that preference goes by expected utility.[13] Here we assume no stronger measurement. These scales need not be hedonic at all. They may not have anything to do with pleasure and pain, or they may.

Adam and Eve each have utility functions that are like a temperature scale family in that their utility functions have an arbitrary zero value and an arbitrary unit. Knowledge of the utility functions by themselves does not allow Adam and Eve to make the common-sense judgment with which we started. Zero points are not a problem, because they want to compare differences: is Adam's decrement in utility due to his washing small in comparison to Eve's increment in utility due to not washing? Comparing differences, choice of zeros for the utility functions wash out. Units are the problem. Choose different units and Eve's difference can be arbitrarily greater or smaller than Adam's. We can assume perfect knowledge of each other's preferences—they know each other very well—but this does not help: Each knows each other's utility function up to zero and unit.[14] But they don't know how to compare units, so they don't know how to make the tradeoff between their utility differences.

---

[11] The setting for this section is meant to call Binmore to mind, especially: Binmore (1994, 1998).

[12] The material for this section is drawn from Narens L. and Skyrms (2018).

[13] See Section 7.1 for a description of Von Neumann-Morgenstern utility theory.

[14] The real world is much more messy, but we want to focus on the problem that remains in this highly idealized case.

13.4 Extended Preferences in the Garden

However, they do make judgments about the tradeoff. Harsanyi showed that this can fit into the framework of orthodox expected utility theory by supposing that they have extended preferences. Adam now has coherent preferences over an expanded outcome set, consisting of old outcomes being Adam's and old outcomes being Eve's. He then has an expected utility representation over all these outcomes on the same utility function. This provides Adam with means to tradeoff of his units with his perception of Eve's. Similarly, Eve has extended preferences over the same outcome set providing her with the means to tradeoff her units with her perception of Adam's. The problem is now that these comprehensive utility scales for these two actors may not agree on tradeoffs. We could suppose that we are all the same under the skin, so that at some ultimate level of description Adam and Eve will agree on tradeoffs. Harsanyi says this, but we find this unpersuasive. We will assume, however, that Adam and Eve can talk to each other about their extended preferences, and their different views of tradeoffs.

13.5 Miscoordinations

Adam and Eve can talk to each other. They can observe miscoordinations. They can discuss them: "But I thought that you really, really minded washing the dishes." "No. not really. I don't enjoy it, but it isn't so bad." Adam and Eve may come to a *modus vivendi* as a result of these interactions, an equilibrium in interpersonal comparisons. They may come to interact as if they could reliably make interpersonal comparisons of utility, and solve coordination problems, like the dishwashing problem, in the manner indicated. As long as this works, they may come to believe that that can make true interpersonal comparisons. But such a view is mistaken, because other *modi vivendi*—other equilibria in interpersonal comparison—could have been achieved. People who hold this view have been misled into believing the objective validity of interpersonal comparisons of utility, even though such comparisons have no objective validity, as Narens and Luce suggest.

In their paper, Narens and Luce raise the question of equilibration dynamics for interpersonal comparisons in a preliminary way, and observe that different starting points may lead to different equilibria. They ask:

- how to characterize a broad class of plausible dynamic rules, and
- how to characterize the class of experiences that ultimately lead to equilibria.

Here we pursue this investigation of dynamics. Adam might judge that it may not make much of a difference to Eve, but a lot to him. Eve may contrarywise judge that it may not make much of a difference to Adam, but a lot to her. Then there is no coordination of who does the dishes. Even though each wants to respect the other's utilities, they disagree on the tradeoffs. The disagreement might even go in the opposite direction, as illustrated in O. Henry's story "The Gift of the Magi" (Porter 1906). Adam and Eve may both want to do the dishes because each believes that the other cares more than they do. Such miscoordinations are seen as errors in interpersonal comparison. Miscoordinations then drive an adjustment dynamic.

It will be useful to regiment our description of the problem. Adam and Eve only care about comparing differences of their utilities with their perceived utilities of the other. Adam has a scale u that is an expected utility representation over all the extended outcomes and Eve has a similar scale v over her extended outcomes. These are only unique up to the choices of zero and unit, but this doesn't matter. It is assumed that Adam has outcomes with maximum and minimum utilities, denoted, respectively, by A_{max} and A_{min}, and Eve has similar outcomes denoted by E_{max} and E_{min}; u defines Adam's view of the comparison of his normalized units and Eve's. Specifically, the tradeoff constant a_0 is defined by,

$$a_0 = \frac{u(E_{\max}) - u(E_{\min})}{u(A_{\max}) - u(A_{\min})}.$$ 13.1

This number is a ratio of differences, so we get the same number whatever scale of Adam's we use—that is, if instead of u in Equation 13.1 another scale $ru - s$ ($r > 0$ and s is an arbitrary real) is taken from Adam's scale family, then Equation 13.1 will still hold. We described this by saying a_0 *is absolute for Adam*. Likewise, Eve's extended utility function gives her an absolute tradeoff constant, e_0, for converting her units to Adam's. (Note that this is the reciprocal of the constant that she would use for converting Adam's utilities to hers.) So we have alternative views on how to convert Eve's utilities to Adam's. The distance between Adam's and Eve's tradeoff constants, $\delta_0 = |a_0 - e_0|$ is thus also absolute.

When Adam and Eve disagree about tradeoffs, they might accommodate by changing their extended utility functions so as to move their tradeoff constants closer together. If Adam moves close to Eve, and Eve moves closer to Adam, we say that they both evince *good will*. They might just split the difference or each might take some different weighted average that gives the other some positive weight. On the other hand, both may lack good will, and move further away from the other. This might, for instance, be for strategic reasons. Each wants to exploit the good will of the other. In this case, the outcome will not be a tacit agreement, but more likely a divorce in the Garden of Eden. Or perhaps Eve evinces good will, while Adam behaves strategically. Then we may get either a divorce or a tacit agreement, depending on how Adam and Eve move. We do not want to just think of averages with fixed weights. The moves might be slow or fast. They might fluctuate in speed, with first relative intransigence and late accommodation. We would like to have a treatment that gives a general, sufficient condition for convergence to an equilibrium of an accommodation dynamics that covers all these cases. For this, we just assume that if there is any difference, they will, depending on the difference, move closer together to reduce the difference. This is formulated formally as follows: For the first disagreement Adam moves a_0 in the direction of e_0 (but not equaling or surpassing it) by choosing a positive real number p that does not depend on Adam's scale and making $a_1 = pa_0$ his new tradeoff constant. Because a_0 is absolute and p does not depend on Adam's scale, a_1 is absolute. Similarly Eve obtains an absolute tradeoff constant $e_1 = qe_0$. Resolving other disagreements then leads to the sequence of absolute tradeoff constants, a_i, e_i, as i ranges over the non-negative integers. This gives rise to an accommodation dynamics that maps the difference $|a_i - e_i|$ into the smaller difference $|a_{i+1} - e_{i+1}|$ except when $|a_i - e_i| = 0$.

Formally, call a function f from the positive real numbers into the non-negative real numbers an *accommodation function* if and only if

(i) f is continuous,
(ii) $f(d) < d$ if $d > 0$, and
(iii) $f(0) = 0$.

An *accommodation dynamics* has an accommodation function f and starts from an initial positive real d_0 producing the *accommodation sequence*, $d_0, d_1 = f(d_0), d_2 = f(f(d_0)), \ldots$.

We assume that $\delta_i = |a_i - e_i|$ is an accommodation sequence with accommodation function g such that $g(\delta_i) = \delta_{i+1}$. Theorem 16 shows that this sequence converges to an equilibrium in which there is agreement on interpersonal comparisons of utility, that is, converges to $\delta = 0$.

Theorem 16 *The sequence δ_i converges to an equilibrium in which $\delta = 0$.*

Proof. The sequence δ_i is an accommodation dynamics. By (ii) and (iii) g has 0 as its only fixed point, that is, 0 is the only solution to $g(x) = x$. Because it is decreasing and bounded by 0, it has a non-negative limit r. Because $\lim \delta_{i+i} = \lim \delta_i$, r is also the limit of the sequence δ_{i+1}. But $g(\delta_i) = \delta_{i+1}$. Thus, r is the limit of the sequence $g(\delta_i)$. But, because g is continuous, $\lim g(\delta_i) = g(r)$. Thus $r = g(r)$, making r a fixed point of g. Because 0 is the only fixed point of g, $r = 0$.

For an averaging example of an accommodation dynamic, suppose that for each i, at the ith stage Adam moves $\frac{1}{8}$ of $|a_i - e_i|$ in Eve's direction and Eve moves $\frac{2}{8}$ of $|a_i - e_i|$ in Adam's direction, and $g(x) = \frac{5}{8}x$ is the accommodation function, but as we have emphasized, this is just a special case.

For each i, (a_i, e_i) is a proper subinterval of (a_0, e_0). Thus by Theorem 16, the a_i and e_i converge respectively to points a and e in the interval (a_0, e_0), where $a = e$. Because the a_i and e_i are absolute, a $(= e)$ is absolute. By appropriately choosing real p_i and q_i so that $a_{i+1} = p_i a_i$ and $e_{i+1} = q_i e_i$, convergence to any point in (a_0, e_0) can be achieved.

The accommodation dynamics and Theorem 16 given above can be generalized in a number of ways. We could have used monotonicity rather than continuity for a technical requirement that covers a slightly different set of dynamics. We could have set the distance at which accommodation stops at some small positive number rather than zero, because it may be close enough for Adam and Eve. The argument is basically the same.

13.6 Three's Company

Suppose that Adam and Eve have agreed that Eve's utilities are multiplied by 2 to convert to Adam's. Now they are joined in the garden by Susanne. Adam interacts with Susanne and they agree that Adam's utilities are multiplied by 2 to convert to Susanne's. Consistency then requires that Eve's utilities should be multiplied by 4 to convert to Susanne's. But Eve and Susanne, interacting separately, may have come to agree on a different tradeoff constant, say 1 to 3. If they all talk together, the inconsistency becomes apparent.

They may restore consistency in various ways. Suppose that the tradeoff between Adam and Eve is already fixed by habit. Then Adam and Eve are on the same utility scale. The question to be answered is where to put Susanne on that utility scale. If Susanne's utilities are multiplied by k to convert to Adam's, they will be multiplied by $2k$ to convert to Eve's. If they all talk, they all know this. They are now in quite a different situation than previously, where they interacted separately.

Adam, Eve, and Susanne may have different opinions about where Susanne should be put on this scale. These opinions can be expressed in terms of conversion to Adam's utilities, as three tradeoff constants, k_1, k_2, k_3. They can now accommodate by repeated weighted averaging—each taking a repeated weighted average that gives everyone's opinions some weight.

If instead, they all moved into the garden at once, with arbitrary extended preferences, their accommodation problem would be more complex. Now for Eve's tradeoff with Susanne, there are six numbers in play, the tradeoff from Susanne's point of view, the tradeoff from Eve's point of view, and the composite tradeoffs through Adam from the four combinations of points of view. You can visualize these numbers on the X-axis, the six numbers for Eve-Adam on the Y-axis, and those for Adam-Susanne on the Z-axis. There is a minimum and a maximum on each axis, and these define a box. The distances between minimum and maximum on the axes, d_1, d_2, d_3, give the dimensions of this box. The box contains all the tradeoffs. Perfect accommodation will shrink each dimension to zero.

Call the distance here the maximum of d_1, d_2, d_3. Then the argument using the accommodation dynamics works here as in the case of two players. It also works just as well for arbitrary, finite numbers of players as for three. If at every step the players responsible for the extreme values modify their views to move these values in the direction of the average, they will converge to an equilibrium.

This line of thinking leads to the following conclusions:

1. A general class of accommodation dynamics converges to a dynamic equilibrium in the case of n agents. as before, there are different possibilities for who accommodates and how.

2. But if n players have already formed a consistent set of tradeoffs, and one new player enters the scene, then the problem is simpler. The existing players already fit on one utility scale, and the question is just

where to place the newcomer. Then simple weighted averaging serves as an example of accommodation dynamics.

13.7 Utilitarianism in the Garden?

If our inhabitants of the Garden of Eden reach agreement on standards of interpersonal comparison, then they have enough to meaningfully employ Sum Utilitarianism. *This does not mean that they must be Utilitarians.* It is possible that they only use their interpersonal comparisons to solve coordination problems. There are interactions in which they might coordinate on multiple equilibria, and in which they all prefer to be at one of the equilibria rather than none, but each has a different favorite equilibrium. They can use Sum Utilitarianism in these situations solely as a coordinating process. That is to say, they can use the comparisons of sums of utilities solely as an equilibrium selection device.[15] If all do so, they will arrive at an equilibrium and each will be maximizing expected utility given what the other does.

13.7.1 Example 1: Coordination in the Garden

Adam, Eve, and Suzanne want to go out to eat together. There are many good eating places in the Garden, and each has a different favorite. Each goes to a place independently. For each of them the worst prospect is going somewhere and not having the other two show up. That would require leaving and searching for the missing one or ones, and would ruin the evening. There are three locations, A, B, C, each Pareto optimal. Table 13.1 shows Adam's extended utilities for himself, Eve, and Suzanne.

Table 13.1 Coordination in the Garden

Location	A	B	C
Adam	1	.9	.8
Eve	.5	.6	.7
Suzanne	.6	.15	1
Total Utility	2.1	3	2.5

[15] In Binmore, all of morality functions only as an equilibrium selection device. But in his theory there are very many equilibria, because he models life as a repeated game.

Adam uses the Utilitarian Sum of his extended utility scale to select an equilibrium, and thus goes to location B, which has the greatest Sum Utility. Since Eve and Suzanne agree with Adam on the values of the tradeoff constant, they must agree that B has the greatest total utility on their own scales, and so they all meet there and have a good time.

Such individuals do not behave as true Utilitarians, because in other kinds of interactions they may not maximize the sum of utilities. For an example, consider the three-person prisoner's dilemma described in Example 2.

13.7.2   Example 2: No Coordination

Adam, Eve, and Suzanne are digging a swimming hole in the garden. Each enjoys swimming but dislikes work. How nice a hole gets dug depends on how many work. Whatever gets dug can be used by all. If two of them dig, the third prefers not to dig but to free ride on the hole dug by two. If one of them digs, the other two prefer not to dig but rather to just splash around in the hole dug by one. If no one person digs, each of the others prefers not to dig either. There is only one Nash equilibrium, in which no one works. But the swimming hole would be so much fun that everyone agrees that everyone pitching in would maximize total utility.

True Social Utilitarians would all work. Those who only use Utilitarianism as an equilibrium selection device would not. This is because true Social Utilitarians do not, on the face of it, maximize individual utility. This requires some explanation lest the whole story become incoherent. For instance, some would have another layer of other-regarding preferences enter the picture at this stage. Adam, Eve, and Suzanne, who use Utilitarianism as an equilibrium selection device, do maximize individual utility. They do so because their utilities depend on what the others do, and the others are using Utilitarianism in the same way. (They exemplify a restricted pragmatic form of Utilitarianism that only uses a Utilitarian Sum in restricted contexts.)

13.8   What Have We Shown?

It all can work out. We have shown that in an austere and difficult case, in which individuals are expected utility maximizers and have only Von Neumann-Morgenstern utilities, conventions of interpersonal comparison can evolve for a wide class of dynamics. We have given a mathematical characterization of the conditions under which this will happen.

With these conventions in place, individuals can use the Utilitarian rule for selection between Nash equilibria of their interactions. And coordination between such equilibria can drive the evolution of such conventions of interpersonal comparison. This is all consistent with expected utility maximization on the part of the individuals, because at a Nash equilibrium each individual is maximizing expected utility given what the other does. In this way, Utilitarianism can be a viable rule for solving coordination problems in a group. Interpersonal comparisons then have a moral status rather than a factual one.

It is, however, not the only way of solving coordination problems. A community of followers of John Rawls would want to coordinate by looking at who was worst off in each equilibrium. To do this, they would have a more demanding problem in setting up a convention for interpersonal comparisons that would allow them to implement their higher level convention of maximizing the minimum gain. On the other hand, the hedonic Utilitarians of the last chapter, in the fortunate realm where all utilities are positive, would not have to arrive at a convention of interpersonal comparisons at all. They could simply maximize the Utilitarian product, which is already meaningful.

14
Where Do We Stand?

We have not set out to evaluate Utilitarianism but to ask what it means. Many philosophers seem to have felt confident in taking on the former without bothering to think very hard about the latter, but Bentham was not one of them. Two different strands of his thinking set the stage for almost all subsequent developments. The first was the use of JNDs, which bloomed into the field of psychophysics. Psychophysics has its own problems, not the least of which begin the problem of multimodal comparisons; but mathematical measurement theory has clarified conceptual issues. Questions about multimodal comparisons of various pleasures, various pains persist. Empirical tests for putting everything on one psychophysical scale, as Bentham had hoped, fail. The psychophysics of pleasure and pain are amenable to scientific study, as Bentham hoped, but the resulting picture will have to be much more complicated than he envisioned. Neurobiology does not simplify everything, but rather magnifies its complexity.

Suppose group options are restricted to those who produce one kind of pleasure, and which produce positive pleasure for everyone. The Utilitarian Sum requires interpersonal comparisons. One kind of Utilitarian (Edgeworth) can say one JND for Mary on her scale counts as much in the sum as one JND for John. This is not a scientific judgment, but rather a moral convention. Given the convention, it then is an empirical matter as to how many JNDs of pleasure a quantity of good will provide for a person. Edgeworth's sexist and racist claims for the superior number of JNDs for Englishmen are subject to empirical refutation. Nevertheless, the convention is sensitive to such differences between individuals where they do exist. This convention gives us one kind of Utilitarianism, applicable in restricted domains.

The other strand in Bentham's thinking involved preferences, which he invoked for different kinds of pleasure and pain on the same scale. Preferences took over in economics, first with the ordinal revolution and then with expected utility theory. Preferences over chancy prospects gives measurement of utility on an interval scale. If all we have are independent interval scales for individuals, then the Utilitarian Sum is, in general, meaningless.

The Pursuit of Happiness: Philosophical and Psychological Foundations of Utility. Louis Narens and Brian Skyrms, Oxford University Press (2020). © Louis Narens and Brian Skyrms.
DOI: 10.1093/oso/9780198856450.001.0001

In that case, all that is left of Utilitarianism is Pareto dominance: if you make some better off and none worse off, then you make society better.

Does the expected utility theory say that you cannot measure utility on a stronger scale? Or does it simply fail to provide a stronger scale? Some care is required here. It is perfectly consistent to imagine a group of individuals whose preferences for some sure outcomes go by a quantity measured on a strong scale, perhaps even one given by JNDs, and whose preferences over chancy outcomes go by expectation. Expected utility theory does not preclude measurement on a stronger scale. But it calls into question the relevance of the stronger scale for choice. Given your utilities over a set of chancy prospects, if you change your utility scale by adding a constant and multiplying by a positive constant, and you choose by maximizing expected utility, you will choose the same.

Within this preference-based expected utility framework, Harsanyi does, and does not, rescue Utilitarianism. He shows that if society has coherent group preferences, and if these respect Pareto dominance, then society's utilities must have a Utilitarian representation. But the theorem does not tell you what that representation should be; there are many. This is just the problem of interpersonal comparison in a different form. Again, this does not tell us that it is impossible to narrow down the choices by other means; it just does not tell us how. Harsanyi had hopes that psychology and physiology could show the way.

It is possible to reunite some of the strands of Bentham's thinking to measure utility on a stronger scale, a ratio scale, by considering preferences over hedonic episodes. If we measure individual's pleasures in this way, we can have a meaningful variant of Utilitarianism. This is Product Utilitarianism, which takes the group utility to be the product rather than the sum of individual utilities. It does not depend on interpersonal comparisons. This again is a kind of local Utilitarianism, applicable in restricted contexts. When we then extend the account to chancy prospects, as in Von Neumann and Morgenstern, there are two natural ways to proceed and they are not equivalent. We have here two more partial reconstructions of Utilitarianism. There is a price to pay for each. One gives up group rationality; the other gives up respect for Pareto dominance.

For each of the reconstructions of Utilitarianism we have the expected utility challenge to answer: how can a stronger notion of utility have any relevance to rational choice. For individual choice against fixed nature, it can't. But in a group setting choice is interactive. What maximizes expected utility for me depends on what you do, and what maximizes expected utility for you depends on what I do. Utilitarianism can then play a role in coordinating group action. For it to function this way, there needs be a social convention that we coordinate on the Utilitarian joint course of action, and a convention as to what we mean by the course that Utilitarianism selects. The convention may require subsidiary conventions. If we are traditional Sum Utilitarians, like Bentham, we need to arrive at a convention for interpersonal tradeoffs. Give sufficient good will and a dynamic accommodation process, this is possible. If we are product Utilitarians, the tradeoff convention is not necessary. We do not see any grand unified theory, but rather a number of alternative, viable, circumscribed Utilitarian approaches.

References

Aczél, J., and Roberts, F. S. (1989). On the possible merging functions. *Math. Soc. Sci.*, 17, 205–43.

Adler, M. (2011). *Well-Being and Fair Distribution: Beyond Cost-Benefit Analysis*. New York: Oxford University Press.

Alper, T. M. (1987). A classification of all order preserving homomorphism groups of the reals that satisfy finite uniqueness. *Journal of Mathematical Psychology*, 31, 135–54.

Alt, F. (1971 [1936]). On the measurability of utility. In J. S. Chipman, L. Hurwicz, M. K. Richter, and H. F. Sonnenschein (eds.), *Preferences, Utility and Demand: A Minnesota Symposium*. New York: Harcourt Brace Jovanovich, 424–36. (*Über die Messbarkeit des Nutzens. Zeitschrift für Nationalkonomie*, 7, 161–9.)

Anon. (1871). Review of Jevons. *Saturday Review*, Nov. 11. (Quoted in Edgeworth 1888 [1881].)

Baily, Samuel (1825). *A Critical Dissertation on Value*. London: R. Hunter.

Bain, Alexander (1882). *John Stuart Mill: A Criticism with Personal Recollections*. London: Longmans, Green and Co.

Baird, J. C., and Noma, E. (1978). *Fundamentals of Scaling and Psychophysics*. New York: Wiley.

Bentham, J. (1830 [1793]). Emancipate your colonies: addressed to the National Convention of France, shewing the uselessness and mischievousness of distant dependencies to an European state. London: C. and W, Reynell for R. Heward.

Bentham, J. (1789). *An Introduction to the Principles of Morals and Legislation*. London: T. Payne, and Son, at the Mews Gate, ch. 1.

Bentham, J. (1822). *Codification Proposal*. London: J. McReery, Tooks-Court.

Bentham, J. (writing as Smith, Gamaliel) (1823). *Not Paul, but Jesus*. London: John Hunt.

Bentham, J. (1843a). Pannomial fragments. *The Works of Jeremy Bentham*. Vol. 3: *Usury, Political Economy, Equity, Parliamentary Reform*. Edinburgh: William Tait, 1838–43, 11 vols.

Bentham, J. (1843b). *The Works of Jeremy Bentham*. Vol. 9: *Constitutional Code*. Edinburgh: William Tait, 1838–43, 11 vols.

Bentham, J. (2013a). *Not Paul, but Jesus*. Vol. III: *Doctrine*. London: The Bentham Project, UCL.

Bentham, J. (2013b). *The Collected Works of Jeremy Bentham: Of Sexual Irregularities, and Other Writings on Sexual Morality*. Oxford: Oxford University Press.

Bernasconia, M., Choiratb, C., and Raffaello, S. (2008). Measurement by subjective estimation: testing for separable representations. *Journal of Mathematical Psychology*, 52, 184–201.

Bernoulli, D. (1954). Exposition of a new theory on the measurement of risk. *Econometrica*, 22, 23–36.

Berridge, K. C., and Kringlebach, M. L. (2015). Pleasure systems in the brain. *Neuron*, 86, 646–63.

Binmore, K. (1987a). Modeling rational players I. *Economics and Philosophy*, 3, 179–214.

Binmore, K. (1987b). Modeling rational players II. *Economics and Philosophy*, 4, 9–55.

Binmore, K. (1994). *Game Theory and the Social Contract I: Playing Fair*. Cambridge, MA: MIT Press.

Binmore, K. (1998). *Game Theory and the Social Contract II: Just Playing*. Cambridge, MA: MIT Press.

Binmore, K. (2008). Do conventions need to be common knowledge? *Topoi*, 27, 17–27.

Birnbaum, M. H. (1990). Scale convergence and psychophysical laws. In H.-G. Geissler, M. H. Mueller, and W. Prinz (eds.), *Psychophysical Explorations of Mental Structures*. Toronto: Hogrefe & Huber, 49–57.

Birnbaum, M. H., and Mellers, B. A. (1978). Measurement and the mental map. *Perception & Psychophysics*, 23, 403–8.

Bridgman, P. (1928, 1931). *Dimensional Analysis*. New Haven: Yale University Press.

Brielmann, A. A., and Pelli, D. G. (2017). Beauty requires thought. *Current Biology*, 27, 1505–13.

Broome, J. (1991). *Weighing Goods: Equality, Uncertainty, and Time*. Oxford: Basil Blackwell.

Broome, J. (2004). *Weighing Lives*. Oxford: Oxford University Press.

Bruni, L. (2010). Pareto's legacy in modern economics: the case of psychology. *Revue européenne des sciences sociales*, XLVIII(146), 93–11.

Camerer, C. F., Loewenstein, G., and Prelec, D. (2004). Neuroeconomics: why economics needs brains. *Scandinavian Journal of Economics*, 106, 555–79.

Campbell, N. R. (1957 [1920]). *Physics: The Elements*. Cambridge: Cambridge University Press. (Reprinted as *Foundations of Science: The Philosophy of Theory and Experiment*. New York: Dover.)

Campbell, N. R. (1928). *An Account of the Principles of Measurement and Calculation*. London: Longmans.

Cantor, G. (1895). Beiträge zur Begründung der transfiniten Mengenlehre (1). *Mathematische Annalen*, 46: 481–512.

Caragiannis, I., Kurokawa, D., Moulin, H. Procaccia, A., Shah, N., and Wang, J. (2016). The unreasonable fairness of maximum Nash welfare. *Proceedings of the 2016 ACM Conference on Economics and Computation (EC '16)*. New York: ACM, 305–22.

Cohen, M., and Narens, L. (1979). Fundamental unit structures: a theory of ratio scalability. *Journal of Mathematical Psychology*, 20, 193–232.

Copeland, A. H. (1945). Review of theory of games and economic behavior. *Bulletin of the American Mathematical Society*, 51, 498–504.

de Lazari-Radek, K., and Singer, P. (2014). *The Point of View of the Universe: Sidgwick and Contemporary Ethics*. Oxford: Oxford University Press.

de Lazari-Radek, K., and Singer, P. (2017). *Utilitarianism: A Very Short Introduction.* Oxford: Oxford University Press.

Diamond, P. (1967). Cardinal welfare, individualistic ethic and interpersonal comparison of utility: a comment. *Journal of Political Economy*, 75, 765–6.

Domotor, Z. (1979). Ordered sum and tensor product of linear utility structures. *Theory and Decision*, 11, 375–99.

Dzhafarov, E. N., and Colonius, H. (2011). The Fechnerian idea. *American Journal of Psychology*, 124, 127–40.

Edgeworth, F. Y. (1879). The Hedonical calculus. *Mind*, 4, 394–408.

Edgeworth, F. Y. (1888 [1881]). *Mathematical Psychics.* London: G. Kegan Paul.

Ekman, G. (1962). Measurement of moral judgments: a comparison of scaling methods. *Perceptual and Motor Skills*, 15, 3–9.

Ekman, G., and Künnapas, T. (1962a). Scales of aesthetic value. *Perceptual and Motor Skills*, 14, 19–26.

Ekman, G., and Künnapas, T. (1962b). Measurement of aesthetic value by 'direct' and 'indirect' methods. *Scan. J. Psychol.*, 3, 33–9.

Ellermeier, W., and Faulhammer, G. (2000). Empirical evaluation of axioms fundamental to Stevens's ratio-scaling approach. Vol. I: Loudness production. *Perception & Psychophysics*, 62(8), 1505–11.

Ellis, B. (1966). *Basic Concepts of Measurement.* London: Cambridge University Press.

Ellsberg, Daniel (1961). Risk, ambiguity, and the savage axioms. *Quarterly Journal of Economics*, 75 (4): 643–69.

Falmagne, J.-C. (1985). *Elements of Psychophysical Theory.* New York: Oxford University Press.

Falmagne, J.-C., and Doble, C. (2015). *On Meaningful Scientific Laws.* Berlin: Springer.

Falmagne, J.-C., and Narens, L. (1983). Scales and meaningfulness of quantitative laws. *Synthese*, 55, 288–325.

Fechner, G. T. (1860). *Elemente der Psychophysik.* Leipzig: Breitkopf und Härtel.

Fechner, G. T. (1887). Uber die psychischen Massprincipien und das Weber'sche Gesetz, *Philosophische Studien*, 4, 215.

Ferguson, A., Meyeis, C. S., Bartlett, R. J., Banister, H., Bartlett, F. C, Brown, W., Campbell, N. R., Craik, K. J. W., Drever, J., Guild, J., Houstoun, R. A., Irwin, J. O., Kaye, G. W. C., Philpott, S. J. F., Richardson, L. F., Shaxby, J. H., Smith, X, Thouless, R. H., and Tucker, W. S. (1940). Quantitative estimates of sensory events. *The Advancement of Science: The Report of the British Association for the Advancement of Science*, 2, 331–49.

Fisher, I. (1892). Mathematical investigations into the theory of price. *Transactions of the Connecticut Academy*, IX.

Foley, D. (1967). Resource allocation and the public sector. *Yale Economics Essays*, 7, 45–98.

Garner, W. R. (1954). A technique and a scale for loudness measurement. *J. Acoust. Soc. Am.*, 26, 73–88.

Gibbard, A. (2008). *Reconciling Our Aims: In Search of Bases for Ethics.* Oxford: Oxford University Press.

Glimcher, P. (2011). *Foundations of Neuroeconomic Analysis*. Oxford: Oxford University Press.

Goldsworth, A. (1979). Jeremy Bentham: on the measurement of subjective states. *The Bentham Newsletter*, March, 3–17. (Reprinted in *Jeremy Bentham: Critical Assessments*, vol. II, ed. B. Parekh. London: Routledge, 1993, 240–54.)

Halévy, E. (1995 [1901]). *La formation du radicalisme philosoplique*, Vols I, II, III. Paris: Presses Universitaires de France. (Nouvelle édition révisée, 1995.)

Harsanyi, J. C. (1953). Cardinal utility in welfare economics and in the theory of risk-taking. *Journal of Political Economy*, 61, 434–5. (Reprinted in Harsanyi (1976).)

Harsanyi, J. C. (1953–4). Welfare economics of variable tastes. *The Review of Economic Studies*, 21, 204–13.

Harsanyi, J. C. (1955). Cardinal welfare, individualistic ethics, and interpersonal comparisons of utility. *Journal of Political Economy*, 63, 309–21. (Reprinted in Harsanyi (1976).)

Harsanyi, J. C. (1976). *Essays on Ethics, Social Behavior, and Scientific Explanation*. Dordrecht: D. Reidel.

Helmholtz, H. v. (1887). Zählen und Messen erkenntnistheoretisch betrachtet. *Philosophische Aufsätze Eduard Zeller gewidmet*. Leipzig.

Hicks, J. R. (1939). *Value and Capital: An Inquiry into Some Fundamental Principles of Economic Theory*, 2nd edn. Oxford: Clarendon.

Hicks, J. R., and Allen, R. G. D. (1934). A reconsideration of the theory of value. *Economica*, New Series, Vol. 1, 52–76; Vol. 2, 196–219.

Hölder O. (1901). Die Axiome der Quantität und die Lehre vom Mass. Berichte über die Verhandlungen der Königlich Sächsischen Gesellschaft der Wissenschaften zu Leipzig, Mathematisch-Physikaliche Classe, Bd. 53, 1–64. (Part I translated into English by J. Michell and C. Ernst (1996). The axioms of quantity and the theory of measurement. *Journal of Mathematical Psychology*, 40, 235–52.)

Hume, D. (1738). *A Treatise of Human Nature*, Book 3, ch. 2. London: John Noon.

Jastrow, J. (1888). The psychology of deception. *Popular Science Monthly*, 34, December.

Jastrow, J. (1896). Psychological notes on slight of hand experiments. *Science*, 3, 685–9.

Jevons, W. S. (1888 [1871]). *Theory of Political Economy*. London: MacMillian & CO.

Kahneman, D., Fredrickson, B. A., Schreiber, C. A., and Redelmeier, D. (1993). When more pain is preferred to less: adding a better end. *Psychological Science*, 4, 401–5.

Kahneman, D., and Krueger, A. B. (2006). Developments in the measurement of subjective well-being. *Journal of Economic Perspectives*, 20, 3–24.

Kahneman, D., and Tversky, A. (1979). Prospect theory: an analysis of decision under risk. *Econometrica*, 47, 263–91.

Kahneman, D., Wakker, P., and Sarin, R. (1997). Back to Bentham: explorations of experienced utility. *Quarterly Journal of Economics*, 112, 375–406.

Kaneko, J., and Nakamura, M. (1979). The Nash social welfare function. *Econometrica*, 47, 423–35.

Kant, I. (1960 [1764]). *Beobachtungen über das Gefühl des Schönen und Erhabenen* [*Observations on the Feeling of the Beautiful and the Sublime*]. Berkley, CA: University of California Press.

Krantz, D. H., Luce, R. D., Suppes, P., and Tversky, A. (1971). *Foundations of Measurement*. Vol. I: *Additive and Polynomial Representations*. New York: Academic Press.

Kreps, D. (1988). *Notes on the Theory of Choice*. Boulder, CO: Westview Press.

Kringelbach, M. L., and Berridge, K. C. (2009). Toward a functional anatomy of pleasure and happiness. *Trends in Cognitive Sciences*, 13, 479–87.

Kringelbach, M. L., and Berridge, K. C. (2010). *Pleasures of the Brain*. Oxford: Oxford University Press.

Krueger, L. E. (1991). Toward a unified psychophysical law and beyond. In S. J. Bolanowski, Jr. and G. A. Gescheider (eds.), *Ratio Scaling of Psychological Magnitude*. Hillsdale, NJ: Erlbaum, 101–11.

Laplace, P.-S. (1825). *Essai: Probabilities*.

Le Merrer, J., Becker, J.Å., Befort, K., and Kieffer, B. L. (2009). Reward processing by the opioid system in the brain. *Physiological Reviews*, 89, 1379–412.

Leknes, S., and Tracey, I. (2008). A common neurobiology for pain and pleasure. *Nature Reviews of Neuroscience*, 9, 314–20.

Lewis, D. K. (1969). *Convention: A Philosophical Study*. Cambridge, MA: Harvard University Press.

Luce, R. D. (1956). Semiorders and the theory of utility. *Econometrica*, 23, 178–91.

Luce, R. D. (1959). On the possible psychophysical laws. *Psychological Review*, 66, 81–95.

Luce, R. D. (1967). Sufficient conditions for the existence of a finitely additive probability measure. *Ann. Math. Statist.*, 38, 780–6.

Luce, R. D. (2000). *Utility of Gains and Losses*. Mahwah, NJ: Lawrence Erlbaum and Associates.

Luce, R. D. (2004). Symmetric and asymmetric matching of joint presentations. *Psychological Review*, 111, 446–54.

Luce, R. D., and Edwards, W. (1958). The derivation of subjective scales from just noticeable differences. *Psychological Review*, 65, 222–37.

Luce, R. D., Krantz, D. H., Suppes, P., and Tversky, A. (1990). *Foundations of Measurement*, Vol. III. New York: Academic Press.

Luce, R. D., and Narens, L. (1985). Classification of concatenation structures by scale type. *Journal of Mathematical Psychology*, 29, 1–72.

Luce, R. D., Steingrimsson, R., and Narens, L. (2010). Are psychophysical scales of intensities the same or different when stimuli vary on other dimensions? Theory with experiments varying loudness and pitch. *Psychological Review*, 117, 1247–58.

Luce, R. D., and Tukey, J. W. (1964). Simultaneous conjoint measurement: a new scale type of fundamental measurement. *Journal of Mathematical Psychology*, 1, 1–27.

Marks, L. E. (2011). A brief history of sensation and reward. In Jay A. Gottfried (ed.), *Neurobiology of Sensation and Reward*. Boca Raton: CRC Press, Taylor & Francis Group, 15–44.

Marshall, A. (1890). *Principles of Economics*. London: Macmillan and Co.

Menger, K. (1934). Das Unsicherheitsmoment in der Wertlehre. *Z. Nationalokon*, 5(4), 459–85. (Published in English as: The role of uncertainty in economics. *Essays in Mathematical Economics in Honor of Oskar Morgenstern*, ed. M. Shubik. Princeton, NJ: Princeton University Press, 1967, 211–31.)

Mill, J. S. (1848). *Principles of Political Economy*. London: John W. Parker, West Strand.

Mill, J. S. (1859). *On Liberty*. London: Parker, Son & Bourn, West Strand.

Mill, J. S. (1863). *Utilitarianism*, 1st edn. London: Parker, Son & Bourn, West Strand.

Mill, J. S. (1869). *The Subjection of Women*. London: Longmans, Green, Reader, and Dyer.

Mitchell, W. C. (1918). Bentham's felicific calculus. *Political Science Quarterly*, 33(2) (June), 161–83. http://www.jstor.org/stable/2141580 (accessed: October 27, 2016).

Moan, E., and Heath, R. G. (1972). Septal stimulation for the initiation of heterosexual behavior in a homosexual male. *Journal of Behavior Therapy and Experimental Psychiatry*, 3, 23–30.

Moore, G. E. (1903). *Principia Ethica*. Cambridge: Cambridge University Press.

Morgenstern, O. (1928). *Wirtschaftsprognose*. Vienna: Springer.

Morgenstern, O. (1976). The collaboration between Oskar Morgenstern and John von Neumann on the Theory of Games. *Journal of Economic Literature*, 14, 805–16.

Moscati, I. (2015). Austrian debates on utility measurement from Menger to Hayek. In *Hayek: A Collaborative Biography*. Part IV: *England, the Ordinal Revolution and the Road to Serfdom, 1931–1950*. London: Palgrave Macmillan.

Moscati, I. (2018). *Measuring Utility*. Oxford: Oxford University Press.

Moulin, H. (2003). *Fair Division and Collective Welfare*. Cambridge, MA: MIT Press.

Myers, A. K. (1982). Psychophysical scaling and scales of physical stimulus measurement. *Psychological Bulletin*, 92, 203–14.

Narens, L. (1981). On the scales of measurement. *Journal of Mathematical Psychology*, 24, 249–75.

Narens, L. (1985). *Abstract Measurement Theory*. Cambridge, MA: The MIT Press.

Narens, L. (1994). The measurement theory of dense threshold structures. *Journal of Mathematical Psychology*, 38, 301–21.

Narens, L. (1996). A theory of magnitude estimation. *Journal of Mathematical Psychology*, 40, 109–129.

Narens, L. (2006). Symmetry, direct measurement, and Torgerson's conjecture. *Journal of Mathematical Psychology*, 50, 290–301.

Narens, L., and Luce, R. D. (1983). How we may have been misled into believing in the interpersonal comparability of utility. *Theory and Decision*, 15, 247–260.

Narens, L., and Luce, R. D. (1986). Measurement: the theory of numerical assignments. *Psychological Bulletin*, 99, 166–80.

Narens, L., and Mausfeld, R. (1992). On the relationship of the psychological and the physical in psychophysics. *Psychological Review*, 99, 467–79.

Narens, L., and Skyrms, B. (2018). Accommodation dynamics for comparing utilities with others. *Philosophical Studies*, 175, 2419–27.

Nash, J. (1950). The bargaining problem. *Econometrica*, 18, 155–62.

Niall, K. K. (1995). Conventions of measurement in psychophysics: Von Kries on the so-called psychophysical law. *Spatial Vision*, 9(3), 275–305.

Nozick, R. (1974). *Anarchy, State, and Utopia*. New York: Basic Books.

Olds, J. (1956). Pleasure centers in the brain. *Scientific American*, 195, 105–16.

Olds, J., and Milner, P. (1954). Positive reinforcement produced by electrical stimulation of septal area and other regions of rat brain. *Journal of Comparative and Physiological Psychology*, 47, 419–27.

Otsuka, M. (2015). Prioritarianism and the measure of utility. *The Journal of Political Philosophy*, 23, 1–22.

Pareto, V. (2010 [1899]). Letter to Pantaleoni. In L. Bruni (ed.), Pareto's legacy in modern economics: the case of psychology. *Revue Européenne des Sciences Sociales*, XLVIII(146), 93–11.

Pareto, V. (1909). *Manuel d'Economie Politique*. Paris: V. Giard & E. Briére.

Parfit, D. (1984). *Reasons and Persons*. Oxford: Clarendon Press.

Parfit, D. (2012). Another defense of the priority view. *Utilitas*, 24(03), 399–440.

Pigou, A. C. (2002 [1920]). *The Economics of Welfare*. New Brunswick, NJ: Transactions Press.

Pitts, Jennifer (2005). Jeremy Bentham: legislator of the world? In B. Shultz and G. Varouxakis, G. (eds.), *Utilitarianism and Empire*. Oxford: Lexington Books, 57–91.

Plateau, M. J. (1872). Sur la measure des sensations physiques, et sur la loi qui lie l'intensité de ces sensations à l'intensité de la cause excitante. *Bulletin de l'Académie Royale des Sciences, des Lettres et des Beaux Arts de Belgique*, 33, 376–88.

Porter, W. S. (writing as Henry, O.) (1906). The gift of the magi. *The Four Million and Other Short Stories*. New York: McClure, Phillips & Co.

Ramsey, F. P. (1926). Truth and probability. In R. B. Braithwaite (ed.), *Foundations of Mathematics and other Essays*. London: Kegan, Paul, Trench, Trubner, & Co., 1931, 156–98. (Reprinted in H. E. Kyburg, Jr. and H. E. Smokler (eds.) (1990). *Studies in Subjective Probability*, 2nd edn. New York: R. E. Krieger Publishing Company, 23–52; and in D. H. Mellor (ed.) (1990). *Philosophical Papers*. Cambridge: Cambridge University Press.)

Rawls, J. (1959). Justice as fairness. *Philosophical Review*, 67, 164–94.

Reid, T. (1785, 2002). *Essays on the Intellectual Powers of Man: A Critical Edition*, ed. Derek R. Brookes. Edinburgh: Edinburgh University Press. (Original work published in 1785. This is the standard edition of Reid's work on the intellectual powers.)

Robbins, L. (1932). *An Essay on the Nature and Significance of Economic Science*. London: MacMillan & CO.

Robbins, L. (1938). A note on interpersonal comparisons of utility. *The Economic Journal*, 48, 635–41.

Rosen, F. (2005). Jeremy Bentham on slavery and the slave trade. In B. Shultz and G. Varouxakis (eds.), *Utilitarianism and Empire*. Oxford: Lexington Books, 33–56.

Russell, B. (1912). *The Problems of Philosophy*. Oxford: Home University Library.

Samuelson, P. A. (1937). A note on the measurement of utility. *The Review of Economic Studies*, 4, 155–61.

Samuelson, P. A. (1938). A Note on the pure theory of consumer's behavior. *Economica*, 5, 61–71.

Sarin, R., and Wakker, P. (1997). Benthamite utility for decision making. Working paper, CenTER, Tilburg, The Netherlands.

Savage, L. J. (1954). *The Foundations of Statistics*. New York: John Wiley and Sons.

Schultz, W. (1998). Predictive reward signal of dopamine neurons. *Journal of Neurophysiology*, 80, 1–27.

Scott, D., and Suppes, P. (1958). Foundational aspects of theories of measurement. *Journal of Symbolic Logic*, 23, 113–28.

Sen, A. K. (1970). *Collective Choice and Social Welfare*. San Francisco: Holden-Day.

Sen, A. K. (1971). Choice functions and revealed preference. The Review of Economic Studies, 38(3) (July), 307–17, https://doi.org/10

Sen, A. (1976). Welfare inequalities and Rawlsian axiomatics. *Theory and Decision*, 7, 243–462.

Sen, A. (1977a). Non-linear social welfare functions: a reply to Professor Harsanyi. In R. E. Butts and J. Hintikka (eds.), *Foundational Problems in the Special Sciences*, Vol. 2. Berlin: Springer, 297–302.

Sen, A. K. (1977b). On weights and measures: informational constraints in social welfare analysis. *Econometrica*, 45, 1535–72.

Sen, A. K. (1979). Utilitarianism and welfarism. *The Journal of Philosophy*, 76, 463–89.

Sen, A. K. (1982). *Choice, Welfare and Measurement*. Oxford: Blackwell.

Shafer, W., and Sonnenschein, H. F. (1982). Market demand and excess demand functions. In K. Arrow and M. Intrillegator (eds.), *Handbook of Mathematical Economics*, Vol. 2. Amsterdam: North Holland.

Shultz, B., and Varouxakis, G. (eds.) (2005). *Utilitarianism and Empire*. Oxford: Lexington Books.

Sigmund, K. (2017). *Exact Thinking in Demented Times*. New York: Basic Books.

Skyrms, B. (1996). *Evolution of the Social Contract*. Cambridge: Cambridge University Press.

Skyrms, B. (2003). *The Stag Hunt and the Evolution of the Social Structure*. Cambridge: Cambridge University Press.

Skyrms, B. (2010). *Signals: Evolution, Learning, and Information*. Oxford: Oxford University Press.

Skyrms, B., and Narens, L. (2019). Measuring the hedonimeter. *Philosophical Studies*, 176, 3199–210.

Smith, K. S., Mahler, S. V., Peciña, S., and Berridge, K. C. (2010). Hedonic hotspots: generating sensory pleasure in the brain. In M. Kringelbach and K. C. Berridge (eds.), *Pleasures of the Brain*. Oxford: Oxford University Press, 27–49.

Steingrimsson, R., Luce, R. D., and Narens, L. (2012). Brightness of different hues in a single psychophysical ratio scale of intensity. *American Journal of Psychology*, 125, 321–33.

Stevens, S. S. (1946). On the theory of scales of measurement. *Science*, 103, 677–80.

Stevens, S. S. (1951). *Handbook of Experimental Psychology*. New York: Wiley.

Stevens, S. S. (1957). On the psychophysical law. *Psychological Review*, 64, 153–81.

Sugden, R. (2004 [1986]). *The Economics of Rights, Co-Operation, and Welfare*, 2nd edn. New York: Palgrave Macmillan.

Suppes, P., Krantz, D. H., Luce, R. D., and Tversky, A. (1990). *Foundations of Measurement*, Vol. II. New York: Academic Press.

Suppes, P., and Zinnes, J. (1963). Basic measurement theory. In R. D. Luce, R. R. Bush, and E. Galanter (eds.), *Handbook of Mathematical Psychology*, Vol. 1. New York: Wiley, 1–76.

Teghtsoonian, R. (2012). The standard model for perceived magnitude: a framework for (almost) everything known about it. *American Journal of Psychology*, 125(2), 165–74.

Thurstone, L. L. (1927). A law of comparative judgment. *Psychological Review*, 34, 369–89.

Torgerson, W. S. (1961). Distances and ratios in psychological scaling. *Acta Psychologica*, 19, 201–5.

Vanderschraaf, P. (1995). Convention as correlated equilibrium. *Erkenntnis*, 42, 65–87.

Varian, H. (1974). Equity, envy and efficiency. *Journal of Economic Theory*, 9, 63–91.

Vazirani, V. (2007). Combinatorial algorithms for market equilibria. In N. Nisan, T. Roughgarden, E. Tardos, and V. Vazirani (eds.), *Algorithmic Game Theory*. Cambridge: Cambridge University Press, 103–34.

Vickrey, W. (1945). Measuring marginal utility by reactions to risk. *Econometrica*, 13, 319–33.

Von Kries, J. (1995 [1882]). Über de Messung intensiver grössen und das sogenannte psychophysiche Gesetz. (Niall 1995, 292–3.)

Von Mises, L. (1912). *Theory of Money and Credit [Theorie des Geldes und der Umlaufsmittel]*. München: Dunker & Humblot.

Von Neumann, J. (1928). Zur Theorie der Gesellschaftsspiele. *Mathematische Annalen*, 100, 295–320.

Von Neumann, J., and Morgenstern, O. (1944). *Theory of Games and Economic Behavior*. Princeton, NJ: Princeton University Press.

Vuurst, P., and Kringelbach, M. (2010). The pleasure of music. In M. Kringelbach and K. C. Berridge (eds.), *Pleasure Systems in the Brain*. Oxford: Oxford University Press, 255–69.

Weiss, D. J. (1981). The impossible dream of Fechner and Stevens. *Perception*, 10, 431–4.

Weiss, D. J. (1989). Psychophysics and metaphysics. *Behavioral and Brain Sciences*, 12, 2.

Weymark, J. A. (1994). Harsanyi's social aggregation theorem with alternative Pareto principles. In W. Eichhorn (ed.), *Models and Measurement of Welfare and Inequality*. Berlin: Springer-Verlag, 869–87.

Williford, M. (1975). Bentham on the rights of women. *Journal of the History of Ideas*, 36: 167–76.

Wundt, W. (1874). *Grundzüge der Physiologischen Psychologie [Principles of Physiological Psychology]*. Leipzig: Engelmann.

Wundt, W. (1883). Ueber die Messung psychischer Vorgänge. *Philosophische Studien*, 1, 251–60.

Zeller, H. (1881). Ueber die Messung psychischer Vorgänge. *Abhandlungen der Akademie der Wissenschaften zu Berlin, philosophisch-historische Klasse*, 3, 1–16.

Zimmer, K. (2005). Examining the validity of numerical ratios in loudness fractionation. *Perception & Psychophysics*, 67 (4), 569–79.

Index

wanting 87
weak ordering 105
    induced by semiorder 109
Weber's Law 43, 45, 111, 125
Weber, E. 43
Weber-Fechner Law 31
Weiss, D. J. 126
Weymark, J. A. 75

Williford, M. 11
Wundt Curve 34
Wundt, W. 33–36

Zählen and Messen 91
Zeller, H. 36
Zimmer, K. 116
Zinnes, J. 100